Civilization

and

Its Contents

Bruce Mazlish

STANFORD UNIVERSITY PRESS

STANFORD, CALIFORNIA 2004

Stanford University Press
Stanford, California
© 2004 by the Board of Trustees of the
Leland Stanford Junior University
Printed in the United States of America

Library of Congress Cataloging-in-Publication Data

Mazlish, Bruce.
    Civilization and its contents / Bruce Mazlish.
        p.   cm.
    Includes bibliographical references and index.
    ISBN 0-8047-5082-3 (cloth : alk. paper) —
    ISBN 0-8047-5083-1 (pbk : alk. paper)
    1. Civilization.   I. Title.

CB151.M29   2004
909—dc22   2004013179

This book is printed on acid-free, archival-quality paper.

Original printing 2004

Last figure below indicates year of this printing:
13   12   11   10   09   08   07   06   05   04

Designed and typeset at Stanford University Press in 11/15 Garamond

Acknowledgments

I have traveled in many climes and civilizations, not to mention times, in the writing of this book. Fortunately, I have had many companions in my journey. Some of their names can be found in the notes; others I wish especially to acknowledge by explicit reference here. For their help in my understanding of China, I am indebted to Peter Perdue, James Pusey, and Dominic Sachsenmaier, as well as to Jonathan Spence, who was kind enough to take time in his busy life to answer a specific query. For insights into Islam, I thank Mehdi Mozaffari and Mohammad "Behrooz" Tamdgidi; for Japan, John Dower; for Russia, Loren Graham; for France, Jeff Ravel. László Kontler and Hugh West were helpful in regard to Georg Forster, sending me papers on him and his role in the eighteenth-century debates about civilization. On the topic of civilization itself, I drew with profit upon the thinking and writings of Said Arjoman, Stephen Mennell, and Medhi Mozaffari.

As every author knows, working with a publisher can make for a different sort of "travel" experience. I have been extraordinarily fortunate in having as my companion in this journey Norris Pope, my editor at Stanford University Press. I cannot imagine a more efficient, understanding, and sympathetic person with whom to work on a book. His talents were first recommended to me by Sophia Rosenfeld, and I wish to thank her and to say that she did not "gild gold" when she described him to me: quite the contrary. In the actual editing of the manuscript I wish to thank John Feneron, the in-house editor, who supervised the overall effort, and Peter Dreyer, the external editor, whose care and erudition have saved me from many errors of both fact and expression.

Contents

Preface

Civilization is an intriguing subject, and for a long time I had been collecting material on it in a desultory way. Then, a few years ago, I received an invitation to participate in a conference to be held the following May in Tehran, Iran. My eye fixed on the word "Tehran," for I had long wanted to visit that city and its country. Without reading further, I mentally accepted. As my eye followed along the invitation, I saw that the conference was on comparative civilizations, sponsored by an Institute for Discourse on Civilization, founded under the auspices of the president of Iran, Hojjatoleslam Seyed Muhammad Khatami. My acceptance grew even warmer.

In preparing my paper, I did extensive research on the origin of the word "civilization." I discovered that it was of Western and fairly recent birth. I shall detail that story later. Then a funny thing happened on the way to Tehran. The conference became embroiled in the political struggles of Iran. A few months previously, the Institute for Discourse on Civilization had participated in a meeting in Berlin that had been marred by a few dissidents rushing the stage, making disparaging remarks, and by a young woman allegedly disrobing in public. This tainted the effort by

Iranian reformers to enter into dialogue with Westerners. The hard-liners back in Tehran seized upon the incident, claimed that that is what happens when you deviate from the fundamentalist position and enter into discourse with the enemy—and arrested two of the institute participants in the Berlin meeting four days before my scheduled conference!

I say "my" conference. In fact, I was one of six American-based scholars who were to participate, and whose papers were to be published in the journal *International Sociology*, edited by Professors Said Arjomand and Edward Tiryakian. They were handling the arrangements from the Western side. Those arrangements were delicate and complicated. The visas, in fact, had not been granted as the conference date approached. Our hosts were too polite to say that given the arrests, the conference was now too dangerous to attend. Only a week or so *after* the scheduled conference had passed did the visas arrive. Very diplomatic! Obviously, we never did get to the conference.

Civilization is clearly a contentious issue. It is not merely a historical subject, awaiting impartial and passionless research and thinking. It is a burning topic, which was made globally so by the UN Declaration of the Year 2001 as the year of the "Discourse on Civilization." It continues to arouse ambivalent feelings in many observers. For some people, it represents the epitome of human achievement, the end result of modern progress. For others, it is a dehumanizing, external threat, bringing with it a mechanization of life and a challenge to "traditional" beliefs. This has been the case from the inception of the word "civilization."

Tehran was the inspiration for going back to the numerous notes that I had already compiled before the invitation. It led me not only to write a paper for *International Sociology*,[1] but to undertake the present book. It coalesced with another stimulus. My title, of course, is a play of sorts on Sigmund Freud's famous book *Civilization and Its Discontents*, which I have used in my teaching for a number of years. Inspired by Freud's book, as by Tehran, I have undertaken to look more closely at the "contents" of the word "civilization"; only after this task is finished do I seek to make tangential evaluations in regard to human happiness and discontents. Also, as is clear, I am concerned with the political as well as the psychological and philosophical implications of the discourse. Furthermore, whereas Freud was a psychoanalyst, I am a historian (although of an interdisciplinary and comparative kind), and approach the topic mainly in that mode of inquiry.

In the light of these inspirations and allegiances, I seek in the book that follows to trace the origins and intentions of the word "civilization"; to pursue its evolution into a form of Western ideology, employed in the service and shadow of colonialism; to treat it as part of what has come to be called the "civilizing process" (following on the work of Norbert Elias); and then to study its spread beyond the West, as it becomes a traveling concept. Then, although briefly, as part of the latter study, I want to raise the question of whether globalization, in the context of a discourse on civilizations, can be regarded as a new form of civilization, with all the problems attendant on both terms, "globalization" and "civilization." At that point, I shall undertake an evaluation and address the question as to the future of the concept of civilization.

A few preliminary remarks are in order. The position I take, claiming only a bit of originality for it, is that the notion of civilization is a social construct. Its political and ideological nature and function have already been touched upon. My historical treatment will show how it changes over time. I want to argue further that there is no "essence" nor "natural" character to be found in what we choose to call civilization. Of course, such an essence or nature can be ascribed to it; this can be one form of its social construction. For example, Oswald Spengler (although he called them cultures) and Arnold Toynbee both treated civilizations as more or less fixed organisms, given to birth, growth, decline, and death. So conceived, they were basically closed entities, little open to borrowings or interconnections.

Such a view is no longer fashionable (except perhaps by the eccentric Samuel Huntington). Most of those who still work with the notion of civilization, such as William McNeill, have liberated it from its fixed boundaries, and are interested in cross-border and trans-civilizational encounters. In fact, some scholars now prefer to think of such interactions as constituent of civilizations, not peripheral and accidental to them. This, it seems to me, is a congenial way of thinking about our topic.

Yet I think that today we must push beyond even this view and perhaps conceive of civilization as an imaginary figure that may itself vanish. The imagination, of course, is not to be dismissed entirely. Rather, it must be recognized for what it is, and then reimagined. As we shall see, the first emergence of cities as the locus of a social community was marked by the construction of walls. These demarcated the division of those who were "civilized" from those without, who were designated "barbarians." If this be acknowledged, then the tearing down of walls around urban centers, a physical manifestation of the advent of "modernity," may be seen as marking a profound shift in the way civilization had to be imagined.

Increasingly, it became hard to imagine a "center" of civilization. Obviously, the concept had become more intangible. And, as the poet Yeats famously remarked, the center cannot hold. Certainly by the eighteenth century, even though that was when the concept was reified, it was harder to imagine civilizations, not only with a center, but as separate and enduring entities. Before that century, it was still possible. Nomads, for example, were yet a potent force; here, then, were the necessary barbarians. Similarly, before the successes of the ages of modern exploration, the physical contiguity of civilizations could be minimized: Japan could seek to shield itself from outside influences.

All this changed by the eighteenth century, and, as I shall try to show, the way was prepared for the coming of the neologism "civilization" in place of the old, simple dichotomy between civilized and barbarian. Once in existence, this reification took on a life of its own, whose ramifications I shall also try to follow. This construction, it must be remembered, took place at the same time as the nation-state was established as the leading form of social bonding. There is, therefore, a dialectic between the two. It embodied a changing relation over time, one in which the nation-state progressively established international institutions and even world-systems.

In this context, we must note that civilizations do not figure as members of international institutions, nor do they "act" and "interact" with one another, except possibly as ideologies. Nor do they mobilize armies, nor raise taxes, nor have representation at the United Nations. Nor do they launch satellites or operate computer banks. Which is not to say that they, or the concept of them, does not have power, indeed, sometimes immense power.

In the chapters that follow, I attempt to explore the origins and nature of that power. For the moment, two aspects are to be singled out. One is that the concept of civilization, developed at the time of the Enlightenment as part of the European imaginary, claimed to offer a universal measuring rod: a civilization had certain material characteristics and it behaved and thought in a certain spiritual manner. (Needless to say, one man's civilization could be another's barbarism.) Certainly this was the case in the past. Was there anything more substantial, however, to the European version of civilization, carrying with it a claim to universality? Or was it a simple expression of domination, to be overthrown in the name of relativism or multiculturalism?

The other aspect to which we must give attention is that civilization is a social-science concept. It is both an attempt to understand and to construct new social bonds. The relevance of this piece of social science to today's problems is not entirely clear. At a time when the process of globalization is apparently accelerating—a matter of some debate—the concept of civilization may simply be outmoded. Such a conclusion can only come from an immersion in the materials, many of them primary, related to our topic.

Even if one chooses not to embrace such a sweeping conclusion, there is a corollary outcome one might want to embrace. It is to recognize that, in a respectful manner, one can take on the task of seeing how different approaches to civility and the civilizing process, in the past and at present, can be compared and perhaps even be reconciled. There is also the possibility that such a comparison might lead to changes in each and every party to the exchange.

By raising a few flags over our line of march, I seek to engage the reader in the historical, sociological, and philosophical inquiry that follows. With these brief comments I hope to entice the reader into joining in the dialogue of ideas that comprise what I am calling the contents of civilization.

Civilization and Its Contents

1

The Origins and Importance of the Concept of Civilization

1

In our contemporary world, the word "civilization" comes tripping off our tongues. It is used in innumerable settings. It is applied to all sorts of past societies, ranging from the Mesopotamian, the Roman, and the Aztec on up to contemporary Western society and its counterparts. We take it for granted that the word has been around since the dawn of—civilization. The extraordinary fact, however, is that the reified noun "civilization," with its accompanying spread as a concept, did not exist before the Enlightenment. It is a neologism of that period. Our first task, then, is to understand how and why this linguistic coinage came about and what the content that stands behind it is.

To do this means distinguishing between the adjective "civilized" and the noun "civilization." For millennia, peoples had differentiated themselves from "others," that is to say, barbarians, by proclaiming themselves civilized or polished. This proud and self-satisfied imaging seems a universal one. We can find it among primitive groups, although the terms "civilized" and "polished" may be missing. It is certainly present among what we have come to call great civilizations, such as the Chinese or the Egyptian. Some version of the dichotomy seems to be essential for peoples trying to mark off their own identity. The exclusion and disparagement of an "other" is a fundamental psychological mechanism by which to achieve this end. Civilization is a form of accomplishing that task.

The manner and times in which this universal piece of human behavior manifests itself is a subject for history. In terms of history, the Greeks are of critical importance for the emergence of the terms "barbarian" and "civilized." It seems that Homer, although he never used the term "barbarian," first made unique use of the epithet, speaking of "bar-bar" speakers, namely, ancient Carian barbarians who, to his ears, babbled.[1] There is a nice irony, as we shall see, in this fact, for it appears that some form of history may be considered a defining quality of civilization. Even from the beginning, a sense of separating myth from history lurks in the background of the belief that one is civilized and thus apart from an earlier state. As we know, history as a "scientific" discipline, offering a sense of secular causality, emerges in the fifth century, with Herodotus. And the father of the new form of inquiry, *historia*, was himself not purely Hellenic, but had been born in Caria, within the province of Lydia, as a subject of the Persian Empire!

Such irony aside, the Greek view of us/them, civilized/barbarian solidified as a result of victory in the Persian Wars of 480–479 B.C. It drew insistently upon the notion of the polis, the city. It was only in the city that one spoke "in public," in a civilized manner, rather than babbling in an uncouth and impolitic tongue. The city, in turn, was based on an agricultural hinterland. The rural and the city thus go hand in hand in the early millennia of the civilized state. This synergy stood in opposition to the anti-Greek, such as the Scythian: nomadic, nonagricultural, nonurban, and uncivilized. Here was the "other" to the Greek, in his purest form.

To us today, the ancient Greek attitude to women, the "other" sex, does not seem very civilized. The female sex was disparaged, and they were lumped along with slaves and children as outside the circle of citizenship. In fact, the Greeks were ambivalent, and the male relation to mothers and wives was filled with tension. One need only think of the plays *Lysistrata*, *Medea*, and *Antigone* to break open the generalization. Still, overall, women in Greek life were backgrounded figures, inferior beings by essence. Having said this, however, we must add that fifth-century Athenians, for example, saw themselves as vastly superior in this respect to the barbarian others, who copulated promiscuously and openly, that is, in an uncivilized manner.

Historical awareness, agriculture, the polis, a more refined treatment of women, such are some of the attributes the Greeks allocated to themselves as "civilized" beings. These attributes become essential elements of the further development of the term and provide reasons for the later claim that ancient Greece was the cradle of Western civilization, when the noun enters common discourse. Their version of what we have come to call civilization rested on the attributes listed above and on possession of a common religion, the practice of shared rituals, and the claim to be one race, with a linguistically defined ethnicity.[2] Looked at more closely, we see that the Greek gods, for example, were partly derived from Near Eastern mythology and philosophy, suitably transfigured and transformed by local usage. Here, at the very beginning, so to speak, we encounter the fact that civilization is always a matter of what, following the example of the term "acculturation," I shall call "accivilization" (using the Latin prefix *ac-*, signifying "toward"), that is, the borrowing of elements from "other" civilizations, while proclaiming one's unique, advanced state and status.

2

Before the arrival of the abstract noun "civilization," there lay at least two millennia of efforts by, in this case, Greeks, Romans, and medieval Europeans, to distinguish themselves from "barbarians" by verbs and adjectives referring to civility and cultivation. Fortunately, there are a number of major scholarly efforts delineating the subject and tracking the usage employed over the centuries in various parts of the emerging Western world.[3] I shall rely heavily on these works, without repeating what they say, but referring the reader directly to them for this part of the history.

I shall instance here only one small part of that story. It concerns the Roman use of the terms *cultus* and *cultura* (it is noteworthy that the Greeks had no such term, referring only to *paideia*, or what would later be called *Bildung* in German). Culture is connected to agriculture, the cultivation of domestic crops. It is what the species wins from nature, thereby setting itself apart. In the process, mankind enters upon urban existence, the division of labor, the creation of a priestly class, and the "cultivation" of the arts and sciences. Written languages come into existence, supplementing the oral as the dominant means of communication. These are some of the characteristics that mark off "civilized" people from "barbarians." Implicit, of course, in this development is a future confusion between the terms "civilization" and "culture."

I want to argue that we must define civilization initially and mainly as a historical phenomenon, rather than seeking to treat the concept in an abstract fashion and then imposing it on the materials. We have to take on the Hegelian task of understanding how self-consciousness as to its own activity came into being. Such a procedure requires us to immerse ourselves in the history of humankind's reflections upon itself and its achievements. In undertaking this effort, I shall focus initially, as I indicated earlier, on the Western concept of civilization, and subsequently broaden my focus.

3

What primarily requires explanation is why the *concept* of civilization—as opposed to "being civilized" or "not being barbarian"—did not emerge until the late eighteenth century. When, exactly, did the reification take place, and why did it occur at that particular time? In his article in the volume *Civilisation: Le Mot et l'idée*, Lucien Febvre declares that he has found no usage of the term before 1766 in any French text.[4] However, as both the *Geschichtliche Grundbegriffe* and Jean Starobinski convincingly argue, the first usage in an accepted nonjuridical sense appears to be in 1756, by Victor Riqueti Mirabeau (the father of the French revolutionary politician) in his *L'Ami des hommes*. It is on this fact that I want to build my analysis of a changed consciousness.

It is puzzling, but little or no attention, as far as I can tell, has been paid to Mirabeau's intentions in using the word, or to the context in which he introduced it. In fact, he uses it only three times in the course of a book of well over 500 pages. In its first occurrence, we are told that "Religion is without doubt humanity's first and most useful constraint; it is the mainspring of civilization" ("La religion est sans contredit le premier et le plus utile frein de l'humanité: c'est le premier ressort de la civilisation").[5] Our initial surprise, then, is that in the supposedly secularizing Enlightenment, civilization is seen as resting on a religious basis.

Our next surprise, on continued inspection, is that the word, attached as it is to religion, first occurs in a chapter on "Work and Money." Here we are told that religion, as opposed to cupidity and luxury, preaches fraternity and softens our hearts. It underlies sociability.

The second usage occurs many pages later. Increasing luxury, we are told, brings an increase in poverty and a decrease in population. "From there one can see how the natural circle leading from barbarism to decadence, by way of civilization and wealth, might be begun again by a clever and attentive minister, and the machine reactivated before coming to an end" ("De-la nâitroit comment le cercle naturel de la barbarie à la decadence par la civilisation et la richesses peut être repris par un ministre habile et attentif, et la machine remontée avant d'être à sa fin.") Here, we are warned of the danger of civilization falling into decadence. The last usage says that "in financial affairs we can see this ghost or specter of barbarism and oppression weighing down on civilization and liberty" ("voyons dans les états de finance ce revenant-bon de la barbarie et de l'oppression sur la civilisation et la liberté").

What are we to make of this birth of the reified term "civilization"? *L'Ami des hommes* itself was published anonymously, caught on immediately, went through a number of editions, and then sputtered out. It was written in haste—six months—and its prose is uninviting; Mirabeau himself boasts of his poor style as the sacrifice made for the truth, which speaks for itself. We must remember further that Mirabeau was one of the leading Physiocrats, and an emphasis on agriculture is the context in which to view his book and his notion of civilization. He was also heavily influenced by Montesquieu, and, as a member of the lesser nobility, was a supporter of the old "feudal" order against the encroachments of the centralizing monarchy.

What else does Mirabeau intend by the term? The subtitle of *L'Ami des hommes* is *Traité de la population*. Mirabeau is concerned with economics as much as morality in his book. He is perhaps the first to embrace the "social question" in its full extent: agriculture, industry, commerce, money, justice, police, manners, luxury, beaux-arts, the marine, colonies, war. Although these topics are treated in a disorderly fashion, the end result is an incipient definition of what constitutes a civilization. It entails a particular form of sociability, which favors increased population, liberty, and justice. Harking back to the original basis of civilization, agriculture, Mirabeau opposes civilization's roots in the city and its future in increased industrialization. In short, the term "civilization" enters the world looking back to an old order and not forward to the coming of the nation-state and commercialized society.

No matter. Mirabeau had loosed upon the world a new concept, which then took on a life of its own. Although the *Dictionnaire universel françois et latin* (or *Dictionnaire de Trévoux*) of 1743, speaks of *civilisation* as a "term of jurisprudence," where it designates a society in which civil law has replaced military law, it remained for Mirabeau to broaden the term so that it referred as well to a group of people who were polished, refined, and mannered, as well as virtuous in their social existence. Within a decade or so, the designation had swept over Europe and become a commonplace of Enlightenment thought. Increasingly, its religious basis was overturned and it became a secularized "apotheosis of reason" (to use Starobinski's term).[6] As such, it also formed part of the idea of progress and became the third phase in conjectural history, signaling the last stage in the movement of humanity from savagery to barbarism and then to civilization. When Samuel Pufendorf, in his *De jure naturae et gentium* of 1672, offered the quintessential account of humanity's development out of barbarism, he did not have available the key word for his terminal point; now it existed, "civilization."

4

Now that we have a deepened idea of how the concept of civilization came into being, with Mirabeau, we can return to the question: why did the reified concept wait to emerge till 1756? The full answer to our question is necessarily overdetermined and multicausal. Moreover, as we have noted, civilization is not a static concept.

The roots of the concept are in the European expansion, starting in the fifteenth century and taking on new life in the eighteenth century with the South Seas explorations. The encounter with new world "primitives" and then Pacific Island peoples evoked the query: how did "civilized" man arise; and this, in turn, required renewed attention to the definition of civilization, as demarcating the last stage of mankind's development from an original barbarism and savagery. I shall go into detail about both the New World discoveries and the South Seas explorations in the next chapter.

Staying for the moment with the general, overall factors leading to the concept of civilization, I want at least to note the role of what can be called the Turkish Threat. For some, 1453, marking the fall of Constantinople to the Ottoman Turks, is more important than 1492 in causing the rise of reflectivity on the self and the other. By means primarily of travel reports, an "occidental anthropology," or ethnography, arose.[7] It moved beyond the

form of the medieval conflict, posed in terms of Christianity being the one true religion that must wipe out its Muslim opponent, to a description of Islam as a "thing," that is, a fact needing
description and analysis in order for the West to defend itself
against its onslaught. Furthermore, it sought to understand this
other by means of categories, such as customs, agriculture, economy, government, and geography, alongside of religion. In short,
it resorted to a new epistemology in order to objectify the other in
whose light it could consolidate its own image as a Christian/
European civilized society.

Thus, for various scholars, the response to the Turkish Threat
in the form of ethnography can be seen as a prime factor in preparing the way for the emergence of the reified term
"civilization." This is an important argument. I wish to qualify it
only by adding that the Ottoman encounter lacked two elements
vital to the formation of a "European" identity. The first is that
the Turkish capture of Constantinople was a land-based challenge that evoked a defensive posture also primarily on land, although great sea battles, such as that of Lepanto (1571), must also
be noted. The New World explorations, in contrast, were maritime in nature, and it was as sea powers that the Atlantic nations
defined their identity, which then merged with that of Central
Europe as it attempted to oppose the Turks with a "European"
identity. The second element emphasizes the expansionary nature
of 1492 and its consequences. As expansionists, the Western nations could both define their own "civilization" and export it to
uncivilized others. Thus, we must reckon with both defensive
and triumphant elements as preparing the way for the emergence
of the notion of Western civilization.

Another source of the concept is the connection with natural
history and the attempt at scientific classification, epitomized in

the eighteenth century by Linnaeus. Zoological and geographical ordering, it appeared, needed to be matched by a similar ordering of men and manners. Montesquieu's emphasis on climate as a shaping force comes out of both concerns and feeds into the discourse about what makes for "civilized" behavior, along with attention to race and the beginnings of social anthropology. In short, civilization becomes part of an inquiry into "natural" history.[8]

More subtly, in the eighteenth century, the debate about civic humanism, and the growing belief that population was increasing, and thus making small republics and their dependence on the virtue of their citizens obsolete, took on a shaping force as well. The political arrow seemed to point in the direction of larger monarchies, and eventually to nation-states based on representation. It was in the absolutist monarchies that space was first allowed for civil society, and thus, by extension, for the notion of civilization as distinct from the state. Alternatively, the emphasis might be placed on culture by some participants in the debate, and thus on the emerging concept of civilization (although as I have indicated earlier, there was to be a tension between culture and civilization). As already noted, concern with population, and thus larger groupings, stands at the heart of Mirabeau's thinking and of his conception of civilization.

Equally to the point is the eighteenth century's concern with mores and manners, as lying at the center of sociability. In our time, Norbert Elias has analyzed how manners, and thus civilized behavior, arose in the context of fifteenth–sixteenth-century court society and then took on bourgeois form in the next two centuries. His now classic account needs to be amended. Thus, C. Stephen Jaeger, in his *The Origins of Courtliness*, argues that the rise of manners preceded the Renaissance and occurred, in

fact, between 939 and 1210 A.D., and as a result of the education
that was increasingly requisite for state and ecclesiastical administrative positions. In this training, individual thinkers and literary artists found a way to tame the violence of the ruling warriors
(a process, incidentally, that continued over the next half millennium). Yet Elias's general thesis holds. As Jaeger himself summa-
rizes it, "When a society educates its members to the extent that
all groups within it willingly make this renunciation [of violence]
. . . then we can speak of civilization, and no longer merely society."[9]

Actually, the issue is more complicated than this, for we must
place both civilization and society in the context of emerging social science. As is well known, it was in the late eighteenth century that the disciplines of the social sciences emerged out of the
matrix of the "sciences of man." The notion of "society" as a
changing entity, constructed by humans not gods, arose mainly
in the late seventeenth century and sparked an extraordinary ab-
sorption with the idea of the social. At this time, Western "man"
realized that his society was not unique, but only one among
many others, and that it itself would change shape over time (by
the nineteenth century, Thomas Carlyle had coined the term
"industrial society" as the successor to "feudal society"). There
was also the awareness that society could be consciously changed
by human reason (although others saw it as changed by unconscious, organic forces).

The belief that rational change was possible helped give rise to
the social sciences, and they, in turn, seem to have supplied the
basis for thinking that change in the desired direction could be
handled consciously and rationally. Merging with the inspiration
of the scientific revolution in the natural sciences, the idea of the
social aspired to its own scientific form, that is, the social sci-

ences. That term itself seems first to have been used in 1789, on the eve of a political revolution, by the abbé Sieyès.

It is in this emerging context that the key words "public," "public opinion," "public sphere," "social" (the *Encyclopédie* was one of the first dictionaries in which the term appears), "social contract," and "sociability" become omnipresent—and along with them the word "civilization." They are all part of an effort to describe, understand, and project new forms of social bonding. They arise in the face of an awareness that the old ties and structures are crumbling when confronted by impending revolutionary change, both political and economical. Gordon S. Wood brilliantly captures what is at work in this situation when he writes that enlightened thinkers like Shaftesbury and Adam Smith sought to understand the social forces, equivalent to gravity, holding humans together in the moral world, which could "match the great eighteenth-century scientific discoveries of the hidden forces," such as magnetism, electricity, and energy, in addition to gravity, that operated in the physical world. "Thus was modern social science born," he concludes.[10] And thus was born the concept of civilization. We cannot understand properly its birth without placing it in the context of the connections problem and the coming of modern social science.

The concept of civilization is also intrinsically tied to the concept of modernity and all that that term entails. The debate that arose at the time concerning culture and civilization is in large part a debate about the merits of modernity, the old battle of the Ancients and the Moderns resumed, in which all the terms are mixed and muddled. Even Kant reflected this fact when he observed: "Cultivated to a high degree by art and science, we are civilized to a point where we are overburdened with all sorts of social propriety and decency. . . . The idea of morality is a part of culture. But the application of the idea, which results only in the similitude of morality in the love of honour and its outward decency, amounts only to civilizing."[11] Opposition to such overcivilization in the form of decadence, already touched on by Mirabeau, and its substitution of artifice for true culture and morality is given classic form, of course, in the discourses of Rousseau.

I shall not pursue here the debates over civilization and its discontents, but rather return to a few concluding remarks as to why the concept itself appeared when it did. I can hardly do better than quote Starobinski again. The word "civilization," he tells us, "gained rapid acceptance because it drew together the diverse expressions of a preexisting concept. That concept included such notions as improvements in comfort, advances in education, politer manners, cultivation of the arts and science, growth of commerce and industry, and acquisition of material goods and luxuries. The word referred first to the process that made individuals, nations, and all mankind *civilized* (a preexisting term) and later to the cumulative result of that process. It served as a unifying concept."[12]

Before concluding this account of the origins of "civilization" as a concept, in which I have been emphasizing the realm of consciousness, I want also to touch on a more immediate and mundane aspect to the origin of the concept. The idea of civilization is, most immediately, a product of the reformist spirit of the Enlightenment. It is set forth as an ideal, a solution to the problems of the absolutist French monarchy. This fact is most obvious in its initial elaboration by Mirabeau. But it is also illustrated by the philosophes in general and especially by the Physiocrats, of which sect the author of *L'Ami des hommes* was a leading member. One need only read his book to see that civilization, with its promise of liberty (retrograde though this might be in Mirabeau's formulation), is offered as the solution to the pressing problems of the day: finance, taxation, commerce, population, foreign policy, and so forth. In short, along with the "universal" aspects of the origin of the concept of civilization, one must keep in mind the particular and local historical circumstances in which it arose.

Stepping back from the immediate, I have tried to add to the elements of Starobinski's summary the longer-range factors of the European exploratory process, the encounter with the Ottoman Turks, the model of natural history, the increase in population and size of social units, the existing reality of improved and refined manners, and the rise of social science and its concepts, with civilization being a prime example of the latter. There remains one other factor of the greatest importance. It reflects a major aspect of modernity. To quote Starobinski again, "The historical moment in which the word civilization appears marks the advent of self-reflection, the emergence of a consciousness that thinks it understands the nature of its own activity, that believes it knows how collective reality develops and ought to be regulated."[13] Whatever its grounding in material, economic developments, and in political and social movements, the concept of civilization in the last analysis emerges out of a changed consciousness and the enlightened human desire to know itself in its most evolved form.

5

I have been arguing that it is in terms of its historical development that we can best understand the idea of civilization. With this conviction firmly established, we can now step back and look at some more abstract definitions, even when the term "civilization" itself is not used. I draw my initial example from Montesquieu's analysis of a nation's constitution, its spirit: as is well known, he stressed the shaping forces of climate and geography, adding to them economic circumstances and the religion, traditions, and character of the nation's people. What the eighteenth-century Frenchman called spirit of a nation, we can well call civilization.

So, too, with the conjectural historian Dugald Stewart, writing some decades after Montesquieu, who declared: "When, in such a period of society as that in which we live, we compare our intellectual acquirements, our opinions, manners, and institutions, with those which prevail among *rude* tribes, it cannot fail to occur to us as an interesting question, by what gradual steps the transition has been made from the simple efforts of *uncultivated* nature to a state of things so wonderfully *artificial* and complicated. . . . Whence . . . the different forms which civilized society has assumed in different ages of the world?" (emphasis added).[14] Here again, although the term "civilization" is not used (even though it is available, for Stewart is writing in 1793), a definition of sorts emerges.

Consider yet another definition from roughly the same period, but this one actually using the neologism. Montesquieu's and Mirabeau's compatriot Constantin-François de Volney writes: "The word 'civilization' is intended to mean the gathering of those same men in a city, namely, in an enclosed area of houses endowed with a common defense to protect themselves against pillage from the outside and disorder from the inside. . . . This gathering carries with it the notions of voluntary agreement from its members, of preservation of their natural rights to have security both of property and person. . . . Thus, civilization is nothing but a social state that preserves and protects peoples and properties." ("Par civilisation, l'on doit entendre la réunion de ces mêmes hommes en cité, c'est à dire en un enclos d'habitations munies d'une défense commune pour se garantir du pillage étranger et du désordre intérieur; . . . cette réunion emporte avec elle les idées de consentement volontaire des membres, de conservation de leurs droits naturels de sûreté, de personne et de propriété; . . . ainsi la civilisation n'est autre chose qu'un état social conservateur et protecteur des personnes et des propriétés.")[15]

These are the voices of some of Mirabeau's contemporaries or near contemporaries. I want to supplement them with some more modern voices. My first instance comes from a scholar studying early modern Germany and what he calls community. In his view, "what is common in community is not shared values or common understanding so much as the fact that the members of a community are engaged in the same argument, the same raisonnement, the same Rede, the same discourse, in which alternative strategies, misunderstandings, conflicting goals and values are thrashed out. In so far as the individuals in a community may all be caught up in different webs of connection to the outside, no one is bounded in his relations to the community, and boundedness is not helpful in describing what community is. What makes community is the discourse."[16] The overlap with our treatment of the term "civilization" is suggestive, with community being a microcosm of the larger discourse that binds.

My next example comes from Samuel Huntington's *The Clash of Civilizations and the Remaking of the World Order* (1996), which offers the following useful definition: "A civilization is the broadest cultural entity short of that which distinguishes humans from other species. . . . It is defined both by common objective elements, such as language, history, religion, customs, institutions, and by the subjective self-identification of people. . . . Civilizations are the biggest 'we' within which we feel culturally at home as distinguished from all the other 'thems' out there."[17]

My last modern example is, I think, the best. It comes from an Iranian scholar who has thought long and hard on the subject of civilization in a comparative frame. He believes that great civilizations consist of "two inseparable parts. The first part is an explicit world vision which can be a set of cultural systems, an ideology or a religion, most often the latter. The second part is represented by a coherent political, military, and economic system usually concretized as an empire or a historical system. I call civilization 'a junction between a world vision and a historical system.'"[18]

Such definitions, which I am calling abstract, catch at the term as it moves through time. What the abstraction aims at is a freezing of the historical flow; I concentrate on studying the flow as best I can, focusing on the experiential origins of the concept of civilization, its emergence as a reified notion, and its subsequent vicissitudes. In this account, one effort, the abstract, supplements the other, the dynamic.

6

Indeed, from the moment of its conceptualization, civilization took on a life of its own, rising above its quotidian origins. As its usage spread, so did its central tenets—and the tensions existing among them. By this I mean that civilization expressed, on one side, a particularly Eurocentric perspective, which in the eighteenth century meant the ideas and ideals of the philosophes; and on the other side, a universalistic measuring rod against which all societies could be compared. In regard to the former, this implied that non-European societies had to become like their European model, or at least as close as possible. In regard to the latter, however, this meant that all societies were forms of civilization, more or less akin to the ideal. It is at this point that relativism and comparative civilization enter the picture.

In this view, civilization is a particular, extended form of cultural-social order and feeling. It is also a deed, a movement, a process. It is necessarily always changing (sometime progressing, sometimes regressing). At the time of its conceptualization with Mirabeau, we can already discern a short list of characteristics. Police is one; as noted by the author of *L'Ami des hommes*, in his stress on civil law, it is an essential element. It entails the subjugation of force and violence to public legality. The latter allows, if it does not foster, a move at least in the European setting to some form of democracy. The embrace of public legality also favors expanding trade and commerce, which requires a stable government and the protection of property rights. Putting aside Mirabeau's dislike of cities, there appears to be an affinity between commerce and urbanity, with each favoring the other. In these cities, the cultivation of manners—civility—is facilitated. In this civilizing process, women play an increasingly important role, and one measure of civilization is alleged by some thinkers, such as James Mill and his son John Stuart, to be the position and treatment of women in the society. And lastly there is, in the original formulation by Mirabeau, an assertion that religion was "the principal source" of civilization, because of the softening of manners.

In the complex of factors that Mirabeau called civilization, sociability and polish loom large. They stand at the center of a concern with civilization as a form of social structure, bonding its members together. In this light, we can see how shallow is the definition given in a present-day dictionary (*Merriam-Webster's New Collegiate Dictionary*): "1 a: a relatively high level of cultural and technological development; *specif*: the stage of cultural development at which writing and the keeping of written records is attained." Even that definition, however, hints at the fact that historical consciousness is the key to the notion of civilization, even if such consciousness is itself based on material change in the form of agriculture and commerce.

I want to emphasize as strongly as I can, however, that the reified word "civilization," first coined by Mirabeau in 1756, and the idea it represents, arose in an efflorescence of modern Western reflection on the bonds that hold peoples together—or apart. For as the pace of material change increased, just before the French and Industrial Revolutions, reflection on the different forms and stages of "connections" linking humans together—or fraying and breaking—became almost compulsive. Once humans become conscious that their relations are socially constructed, even if mostly unintentionally, they are haunted by that awareness. Not surprisingly, civilization is a part of that modern obsession, with momentous consequences for how humans conceive of themselves and for how they relate to others.

2

Civilization as Colonial Ideology

1

Within a decade of the employment of the term *civilisation* in this new sense by the elder Mirabeau, use of it with this meaning was widespread. As suggested in the previous chapter, for some, it meant a singular European achievement, to which lesser peoples could only aspire and possibly copy in part. For others, it meant a form of social and cultural organization that could take, and had taken, varied shapes. Peoples other than Europeans could also have civilizations of more or less equal worth. However, even if these others were admittedly in possession of civilizations, some Westerners relegated them to second-class civilizational status. As can readily be seen, various permutations and degrees of universalism and relativism were possible.

An additional complication arose almost from the beginning. It concerns the rise of the modern concept of "culture" shortly after the advent of the concept of civilization, as a reaction to it. We have noted the Roman attitude to culture, the cultivating of the land, as a prelude to the idea of being civilized and living in cities. Culture, in this early sense, and the later idea of civilization seem adjunct notions. Yet implicit in their historical trajectories is an ambiguity of meaning and an opposition. Both outcomes manifest themselves in the period immediately after Mirabeau's first use of the term *civilisation* to signify what "civilization" now implies.

What happened is that, for many people, "civilization" came to mean the cold, calculating, mechanical, and universalizing way of thinking embodied, supposedly, in the Enlightenment and in revolutionary France. Culture, on the other hand, as enunciated, for example, by the German philosopher Johann Herder in the 1780s, is seen as rooted in the blood, land, and unique history of a particular people, the *Volk*. Between *Volk* and humankind, a gulf is opened up. It was made specific with the invasion of the German states by the French revolutionary armies at the time. Interpreted in this light, civilization is merely material, while culture is mainly mental and moral, and as much about the individual's development (*Bildung*) as that of his or her society. In the end, then, the two concepts could be freighted with different meanings just as often as they were used as synonyms.

In fact, the two terms are like star-crossed lovers. Both emerge out of the desperate urge to restore meaning to societies experiencing the breakdown of connections brought by modernity around the end of the eighteenth century. Both describe a way of peoples relating to one another. Then, more often than not, their existence becomes complicated and frequently antagonistic. Where culture, as in agriculture, first starts out as a basis for the emergence of civilization, it quickly refuses to follow along with the latter in an embrace of science and technology and a heightened consciousness of modernity. Instead, it turns back to the land—blood and roots—and holds dear that which is unique, and, if possible, restricted to a small group. Over the course of the

next century, the nineteenth, "culture" became the core definition of a new discipline, anthropology, and moved away even
further from its companion term "civilization."

As I return to my focus on civilization, the love-hate relation
to culture must be kept in mind. This will become clearer, and be
demonstrated specifically, as I examine the way in which Mirabeau's original conception was carried out into the rest of the
world. It became an intrinsic part of what I am calling a colonial
ideology—that is, the use of the concept of civilization to justify
domination and superiority over others. As we shall see, however,
such hegemony is a puzzled one, marked from the beginning by
doubts and often a guilty conscience. And by opposition in the
shape of culture. That, too, is an intrinsic part of civilization.

2

There are many parts to the story to be told. My account will be
selective. I shall devote attention specifically to the explorer Captain James Cook, the anthropologist Georg Forster, and the
British ambassador Lord George Macartney. Two are British and
one is German, but their views can be taken as representative of
some of what was happening in regard to the experience of civilization by numerous Europeans. The framework in which I shall
place them includes both the New World and the South Seas discoveries.

It will be useful before engaging with this subject to speak
briefly about the general topic of frontiers and boundaries. One
definition of frontiers is that they draw a line between competing
powers, a line that nevertheless does not prevent trade. In fact,
trade flows across such frontiers. Boundaries, on the other hand,
are simply geographical markers, cutting off one group from an-

other. As with borders, boundaries, in the words of one scholar, "imply division but they do not imply interaction in the way 'frontier' can."[1]

If we can accept this distinction, then we can see that "frontier" is a useful concept in regard to civilization. In its usual form, it embodies the idea that "we" are civilized, while those on the other side of the frontier are barbarians. Such an idea could effectively support a ruler's claim to authority over a particular domain, by fostering, as we are told, "antagonism towards the neighboring group or groups, chiefly through the creation, revival, and maintenance of ideologies, with their accompanying myths and symbols, that emphasized the uniqueness of the in-group and a negative picture of the out-group."[2] The largest form of such ideology is "civilization."

Long before the reification of the term "civilization," we encounter intimations of its claims as a form of dominion. A major example of this situation is the medieval division between the Islamic and Christian worlds. One of Europe's earliest attempts to define itself involves the putting forth of an exclusive creed (matched by one on the other side of the frontier). The frontier itself, over time, kept shifting; one thinks of the jihads and Reconquistas. Christianity as a unifying force in the West (no matter how divided in fact internally) required fixity, however, and total separation from its Islamic opponent across the frontier. The scholar I cited earlier speaks anachronistically of "contending civilizations."[3] This portrayal suggests that to know what I am, I must know that I am not this "other." Given such a conviction, it is then only by conquering the other and incorporating him in one's own creed and culture, rather than by accommodation, that one can break out beyond one's own frontier and "civilize" the

barbarians on the other side. Conquest and civilizing become
synonyms; and in the case of Europe, both become entwined
with the spread of Christianity.

The other element besides frontiers concerns the settled areas,
especially cities; here is where civility is best exhibited. Barbarians
exist outside urban centers and their urbanity, and they must be
brought carefully within the walls. Nomads, by definition, are
uncivilized, whether they are Mongolian "barbarian" invaders
from a nomadic-pastoral world into the Ottoman Empire or native Indians, wandering in the wilds of the New World. It should
come as no surprise that the Spaniards as quickly as possible laid
out streets and squares in their new frontier possessions in the
"belief," as we are told, "that cities were synonymous with civilizations."[4] In the process, of course, the frontier becomes incorporated into the home civilization.

3

The first episode in our account of the travels and travails of civilization involves the so-called discovery of the New World and
the role that that exploratory effort played in defining the Old
World. As I have already argued, this phase of European expansion is one of the reasons in back of the emergence of the concept.
Happily, we have a wonderful guide in the shape of J. H. Elliott's
The Old World and the New, 1492–1650. Elliott's most general aim
is the same as mine; as he remarks in his preface, he has written
his book "to encourage the discussion of broad issues which relate
to the general history of civilization."[5] Restricting himself to the
period of early modern history, Elliott shows in detail how the
Europeans entered upon a new frontier and confronted beings of
whom they had previously had no knowledge. Were such beings
truly human? In seeking to answer that question, it was necessary

to look more intently at oneself and one's own form of society. As Elliott contends, "This process of reappraisal was supremely important, because it gradually forced Europeans to move away from a narrow and primarily political definition of 'civility' towards the broader concept of 'civilization.'"

He immediately adds, "which was not necessarily equated with Christianity." The fact was that many saw in the Indian a being superior to their European counterparts, a "noble savage" as Rousseau would describe him much later. In this description, Rousseau was echoing his earlier compatriot Montaigne, who in his essay *Des cannibales* turned classifications such as "savage'" or "barbarian" upside down and made them more applicable to the supposedly "civilized" Europeans than to the Indians. In this perspective, it was the conquistadors who were violent and savage, animated by the most sordid motives of lust and greed. Yet they claimed to be Christians. As Elliott describes the author of the *History of the Discovery of the Indies* (1528), Fernàn Pérez de Oliva, "By emphasizing their [the Indians'] fortitude and nobility of character, he effectively points the contrast between the innocence of the alleged barbarians, and the barbarism of their supposedly civilized conquerors."[6] In this context, Christianity, rather than being a civilizing force, is a force for evil. It is equated with conquest, with the Indians being nailed to the cross.

In fact, of course, this was a minority view in a debate that swirled back and forth. While many in the Catholic Church sought to protect the Indians, arguing for their humanity, and the possibility of their salvation by the true faith, just as with their European counterparts, many more, in both Church and state, saw the Indian as a barbarian, possibly a subject for conversion, but definitely a subject for exploitation as an uncivilized savage. Whatever the arguments, the contest on the ground was won largely by the holders of the latter view. Nevertheless, this element in the emergence of the notion of civilization was tinged with bad conscience. Christianity and its "civilizing mission" became the ideological salve to justify early European imperialism. As Elliott concludes, "the doubts and the guilt were held in check by the firm conviction of the superior merits of Christianity and civility."[7] The argument as to whether Christianity was a vital part of the concept of civilization persisted for a long time, as did the growing conviction for some that it was, in practice, as barbarous a religion as the ones that it sought to displace.

For our purposes, there are two further points of special importance. The first is that sixteenth-century Europe, as it came to grips with the realities of America, saw itself as in a mirror, however distorted, as something that would eventually be called a civilization. Europe's identity, with its strengths and weaknesses, was shaped by its reflection in the image of the other, the Indian. It could only recognize itself as the Old World when confronted with a New World. In this new geography of self, it could also place its civilized state in the midst of the continents, at the center of the newly discovered globe. Noting that the river Guadalquivir in Cordova gave access to the sea, Pérez de Oliva declared that "formerly we were at the end of the world, and now we are in the middle of it."[8]

The other point is that this new self-knowledge involved, as already noted, the development of an incipient social science: anthropology. Confronted with "other" humans, explanation was desired in secular, as well as religious, terms. How to explain the differences between peoples? Was it merely geographic and climatic? Or was it mainly a question of "civility," carrying with it the notion of different degrees of barbarism, as Bartolomé de las Casas argued in his *Historia de las Indias*? If the answer was in "civility," its aspects must be investigated more closely, which meant attention to its roots in agriculture, the city, the trade linked to the latter, and other characteristics.

Moreover, the very governing of the "barbarians" entailed the need for some understanding of the customs and traditions—the culture—of those being ruled. Whether for officials intent on taxing their subjects or missionaries aspiring to convert them, knowledge was required of the "knowledges" possessed by the subject peoples. It was a short step from this necessity to an inquiry into comparative "cultures"; and from thence, with the addition of philosophical and scientific curiosity, potentially to comparative "civilization."

That inquiry went forward in terms of history, philosophy, religion, and an early form of anthropology.[9] As an emerging discipline, the latter challenged the abstract and metaphysical effort to decide what was human—the universals—with an empirically oriented approach to both the universal and the relative. It struggled to free itself from philosophy by concrete examples of the diversity of humankind, and from religion by recognizing competing variants—comparative religion—or, taking a further step, the emancipation from any particular religious conviction and the embrace of secularism. The New World, in short, was an important midwife in the birth of a new science. What is more, in any and all of its manifestations, the emergence of anthropology as a separate study, a new social science, henceforth constituted a lasting feature of what would come to be called civilization. It is in its deepest aspect a part of the self-reflexivity that creates the concept.

4

A distinguishing feature of European civilization in its early manifestations was its expansionism and exploratory zeal. In the sixteenth century, this took the form mainly of maritime expeditions. The "discovery" of the New World was one consequence. Another was the first circumnavigation of the globe ever by humans: Magellan's voyage of 1519–21. This momentous event marked European society off from all others, although eventually bringing the others into a global network of connected nations. It was not that other nations couldn't have engaged in similar explorations; for example, the Chinese in the period from about 1414 to 1433 mounted a much larger fleet than Columbus's—with over a hundred and fifty vessels to his three, and of immensely greater tonnage—with which to enter the Indian Ocean, but they were called back for reasons of internal politics and disposition. It was simply that the Westerners were steadily driven by economic greed, missionary desires, and emergent scientific curiosity to go over the edge.

We have seen the results in regard to the New World. By the eighteenth century, these efforts were turned to the South Seas, and the second great wave of overseas exploration was undertaken by the Western powers. This becomes the second episode in my exploration of the coming of civilization.

To be sure, long before Magellan had entered the area in 1520, Polynesian navigators in their open-sea canoes had explored the South Seas and settled many of its numerous islands. Never, however, did they seek to "invade" other parts of the globe, nor could they have done so with their existing technology. More or less the same conclusion must be drawn, technology aside, for the Chinese. The Europeans, however, were not so inhibited, and they followed upon Magellan's circumnavigation with further explorations a few centuries later. It was a truly "European affair," in the sense that subjects of many countries engaged in the effort: Russians, French, Dutch, Portuguese, and especially the British.

The British effort, in particular the *Voyages* of Captain Cook, 1768–79, becomes my text for a further inquiry into the content of civilization. As is clear from the dates of Cook's voyages, he wrote his volumes a decade or so *after* the concept of "civilization" had been born with Mirabeau. A glance at almost any page of the *Voyages* will also show that he put down his thoughts in the context of the Enlightenment. In short, a recognized form of European civilization already existed. What my reading of the *Voyages* will attempt to do is probe what that civilization saw itself as being in the mirror of yet new encounters, further defining Europe's notion of itself. And, of course, of further others.

I speak of Cook's account of his voyages. In fact, the published account is problematic, with other hands engaged in its writing and publication. Much scholarship has been expended in establishing the facts in this regard. For my purposes, however, I need only acknowledge the problem and then proceed to write of "Cook" as if he were the sole voice of the account of his voyages. He is certainly the iconic figure in this story, just as Columbus was in the first wave of discovery. The French might argue, for example, for Bougainville, but he, along with many other contemporary explorers of the South Seas, is a less prototypic version of Cook.

With Cook we have front and center a special, distinguishing feature of the second round of explorations. In addition to the usual motives of charting the seas and possessing new lands, politically and religiously, there was a powerful desire to acquire new, scientific knowledge. In between Columbus and Cook, the Scientific Revolution occurred. Cook's first voyage in 1768 was co-sponsored by the Admiralty and the Royal Society. Its stated objective was to observe the transit of Venus across the face of the sun in 1769 by setting up an astronomical station at Tahiti. In addition, on board was Joseph Banks, a wealthy botanist and future president of the Royal Society, with four assistants and much scientific equipment.

On the second voyage (1772–75), Cook was accompanied by a professional astronomer, a noted painter, and, most important for our purposes, a learned scientist, Johann Reinhold Forster, and his son Georg, early anthropologists. In his instructions for the second voyage, Cook was enjoined to make "observations of every kind, as might be useful either to navigation or commerce, or tend to the promotion of *natural* knowledge" (emphasis added).[10] Here we have one highly important part of the content of European civilization.

Of equal importance is the second half of Cook's instructions. "I was also directed," he tells us, "to observe the genius, temper, disposition, and number, of the inhabitants, if there were any, and endeavour by all proper means to cultivate a friendship and alliance with them; making them presents of such things as they might value; inviting them to traffic, and showing them every kind of civility and regard." We have here another part of the content of European civilization: its concern with *human* knowledge, the purpose of the Forsters' inquiries, which, incidentally, contributes to a better understanding of what is involved in the concept of civilization. Cook's instructions also speak of showing civility to the natives. What is not stated is that his voyages are intended to bring civility *to* the natives as well. In short, a clearer conception of European civilization is joined to an intention of bringing that civilization to those less civilized.

It was the technological and scientific achievements of European civilization that made the voyages possible. Great advances in boat building, although not necessarily in size, were required, such as deep keels. And, of course, guns with which to establish dominion over large groups of natives equipped with "primitive" weapons. Navigational aids were requisite, ranging from astrolabes to chronometers (finding one's longitude was still problematic). Mapping was essential. Indeed, maps were a prime means of establishing the nature of European civilization, guiding explorers such as Cook in the directions they were to go, and often being a major reason for the voyages, that is, the need to improve existing maps. Maps also marked the expansion of European civilization, for lands that were taken possession of had to be so indicated by visual representation. Lines drawn on a map fixed boundaries, accompanied by the imposition of names upon them. In a typical move, Cook planted a post in South Island and "hoisted upon it the Union flag and honoured this inlet with the name of Queen Charlotte's Sound."[11] The natives standing by, and their customary names, were simply ignored.

It was not only advanced technology and an eye for mapping that Cook and Banks brought with them on the first voyage. They also carried the scientific way of thinking. The account of the voyages is filled, for example, with inferential reasoning. An instance among many is Cook's observation of large billows from the north, of which he declares: "These billows never ceased with the cause that first put them in motion; a sure indication that we were not near any large land and that there is no continent to the south, unless in a very high latitude."[12] Now, in itself, inferential reasoning is to be found in other cultures; one thinks of what is called Zadig's method, which can be found among hunter-gatherers long before the arrival of Europeans. What is characteristic of eighteenth-century civilization, however, is the insertion of inferential reasoning into a formal scientific method. This required its linkage to facts. "But this was too important a point to be left to opinions and conjectures," Cook continues. "Facts were to determine it and these could only be obtained by visiting the southern parts." Facts were, in turn, connected to sense observations; as Cook declares at one point: "I had the demonstration of my sense to satisfy me that they were not real yams." The Royal Society's sponsorship had not been in vain!

It was also in the spirit of the Royal Society that, as we are told, Banks desired to know more of nature than was to be found in books (although the latter would be one result). As indicated earlier, such knowledge was in the form of natural history. It was to be accompanied by what may be called human history as well. As the editor of the *Voyages* tells us, an aim of the expedition was greater knowledge of the countries and peoples encountered, "their productions, manners, customs, religion, policy, and language."[13] On one hand, Banks, for example, wished to "enrich his native country with a tribute of knowledge from those which have been hitherto unknown." On the other hand, he was "not without hope of leaving among the rude and uncultivated nations that he might discover, something that would render life of more value, and enrich them perhaps in a certain degree with the knowledge, or at least with the productions, of Europe." To this latter end, sheep, goats, and cattle were often left with the islanders, in the hopes (generally vain in the outcome) that they would breed and retain them.

Civilization entailed a two-way traffic. It defined itself by learning about its differences from others "hitherto unknown." At the same time, it carried with it—some might say imposed—what it "was" on "rude and uncultivated nations." There is, therefore, a tension in this idea of civilization. Other nations without the new concept, even those that were "civilized," lacked the self-awareness and reflectivity, as well as the ambivalence, that

are made manifest in accounts such as those of Cook's voyages in the later eighteenth century. This is the spirit, for example, in which the question long debated in philosophy as to nature and nurture is tackled—"Whether the shame attending certain actions which are allowed on all sides to be in themselves innocent, is implanted in Nature or superinduced by custom?"[14] The *Voyages* is one long disquisition on this topic, working by empirical rather than abstract reasoning. In the end, the question really concerns civilization, which is, in fact, a highly reified version of custom, to which is added man's working on nature, that is, his material achievements. In this light, civilization is the highest, most refined, and most complicated form of nurture.

All the particular observations that follow are to be judged in the context of the generalization just made. One theme running through Cook's account is trade. Navigation itself, and the charting of new lands, was in the service of Britain's desire to expand its trading empire. As it turned out, rude and uncultured peoples in the South Seas were poor suppliers and customers. At one point, Cook remarks of the people on Mollicollo Island that they set no value on nails or any other sort of iron tools, "or anything we had."[15] Under such circumstances, it was difficult to obtain by appeals to self-interest the produce, water, or wood needed by the mariners. Instead, benevolence was more likely to produce a pig (although perhaps, Cook speculated, it might have been given as a peace offering).

Mostly Cook records his impressions and does not indulge in reflections of the sort I have suggested above. Yet the judgments and valuations are always underneath the observations. One tribe has no sense of private property. Another tribe, Cook speculates, does. What is common to both observations is Cook's assumption that private property is a sign of higher cultivation. This is

the background for his frequent, almost obsessive, reports of thieving on the part of the natives. In their rude state, such natives obviously have no respect for private property. If it isn't nailed down, and sometimes even then, it is fair game for appropriation. The perpetrators needed to be caught, and to make restitution. Here was a clash of values that eventually led to Cook's death, whose initial cause was the stealing of a cutter.

Trade is part of the larger concept of exchange. It is one mode, of which understanding is another. Both come up against the language barrier. Earlier, in the New World exchanges, this had been a problem, vividly represented in the difficulties of Cortés, for example, in finding translators. Cook had the same problem across the South Seas, where an interpreter might be competent in one set of languages but ignorant a few islands over. How to understand the "other" if one cannot understand the language? Sign language could go only so far. And as far as understanding the natives' customs, command of the tongue was essential. Cook does not treat natives as "babblers," that is, barbarians mouthing uncouth sounds, as did Homer centuries earlier. European civilization is interested in understanding its "others," which means acquiring foreign languages rather than merely disparaging them.

There was little empathy among the early Greeks. Hermeneutics, the art of interpretation, may derive from the Greek god, Hermes, the messenger, but civilized Greeks had scant interest in interpreting the verbal texts of "others." That task, mainly directed to written texts, fell to the scholars of the early modern West and their followers. From the sixteenth and seventeenth centuries on, hermeneutics is an essential feature of civilization in its European form. In turn, an essential part of hermeneutics is empathy, the desire to see the other's point of view—for how else

to understand him? Thus, in a surprisingly modern vein, Cook empathizes with the native's suspicion: "I consider the light in which they must view us. It was impossible for them to know our real design; we enter their ports without their daring to oppose . . . by the superiority of our firearms. Under such circumstances, what opinion are they to form of us?"[16]

In a similar mode, Cook is constantly drawing comparisons between native and European mores and manners, and not always to the advantage of the latter. Thus, he seeks to understand the natives' religion, praises their sagacity in foretelling the weather, recognizes the superiority of their fishing gear to his own, and compliments them on other of their practices. Their occasional openness to new ways is contrasted with his own crew's rejection, as an unacceptable innovation, of Cook's prescriptions for preventing scurvy. He even treats the Tahitian practice of taboo with respect and understanding.

Yet his attitude is basically divided to the point of being schizophrenic. It also seems to vary over time. He praises, for example, the Hawaiians for their "consciousness of their own inferiority; a behaviour which equally exempts their national character from the preposterous pride of the more polished Japanese, and of the ruder Greenlander."[17] In short, they know their place. Nakedness on many of the islands affronts Cook. Clothes, for him, are clearly essential for civilization (or what Thomas Carlyle would identify as culture). Lack of decent covering was connected to sexual promiscuity, which Cook also saw as a mark of the savage state. (Others, of course, such as the Frenchmen Bougainville and Diderot praised such freedom from bourgeois morals.) When the natives demonstrate stratification practices, Cook praises them for this mark of civilization. On the other hand, in an unusual slip, he refers to the New Zealanders as "Indians," placing them with the inferior beings of the New World. Reversion to revulsion is always just below the surface.

A primer for the latter attitude is cannibalism. As Cook says, "we were struck with horror," when viewing the bones of a human body picked clean. Evidence was everywhere and repeated, as was Cook's repulsion. Yet in a sudden insight, commenting on the clear proof of New Zealand cannibalism, he remarks, "consider what a savage man is in his natural state and even after he is, in some degree, civilized. The New Zealanders are certainly in some state of civilization [a description itself of much interest for our purposes]; their behaviour to us was manly and mild," and they possessed some arts.[18] Implied is the subconscious knowledge that civilized man is capable of uncivilized behavior as well. Before Freud, Cook voiced the knowledge that civilization is a thin veneer over nameless passions.

For some thinkers, including Mirabeau, religion is the basis of civilization, for it softens the passions. Although Mirabeau's contemporary, Cook was closer to the Enlightenment position on religion, and took a more skeptical and secular view, observing in regard to the Tahitians: "Of the religion of these people, we were not able to acquire any clear and consistent knowledge: we found it like the religion of most other countries, involved in mystery and perplexed with apparent inconsistencies."[19] In addition, Cook brought to his remarks on the subject tolerance and the attitude of a participant observer, for example, sitting in on some of the native ceremonies.

There is an irony, then, in the circumstances of Cook's murder in Hawaii. Although the subject is shrouded in controversy, it appears that Cook may have become an object of adoration to the natives. Treating him as a god, or so it is alleged—for example, arraying their idols with red cloth "in the same manner as was done to Captain Cook,"—they eventually turned on him and, in fact, devoured him.[20] It was all an accident, it appears, connected to thievery. The natives had stolen a cutter, Cook's men had responded by unintentionally killing a chief and threatening to take the king, whereupon the natives, unafraid of the European guns, had overwhelmed Cook's small force and killed him. Caliban had turned against his master.

I could go on with more details, but I want now to draw a line under our observations, based on Cook's account of his voyages. What we witness in each of his island forays is an encounter between "civilization" in its British incarnation and an "aboriginal" population. The latter may be rude or sophisticated, but the result was the same. Neither population had ever even seen the other previously: the natives had never encountered white men before, nor the British the natives before the coming of the ships.

What did each think of the other? We have almost no evidence in regard to the natives. We know almost nothing of how they passed on knowledge of the encounter; it was certainly not in writing, of which they had no possession. We know little about what the natives, often naked themselves, thought of the clothed white men (no women, of course, were along).

The situation is entirely different with the Europeans. Cook's account is one long exploration, not only of the islands but of its inhabitants. He took possession, not only of land, but of the natives as well, even if only in the form of knowledge about them (flawed as it might be). In some cases, natives were actually brought back to England as curiosities, living evidence to match the artifacts collected for exhibit in museums. In another manner, they were embalmed, so to speak, in Cook's written account, available to all in a "future age."

The encounter was decidedly one-sided. What of accivilization? Mostly, it appears, European civilization was imposed on
the natives, in the form of actual physical domination or of intellectual and cultural superiority. It was like the boomerang discovered by Cook as part of Australian tool use, recoiling upon the
native. For the European, it was a matter of selecting what pieces
of native existence might be useful "back home." In the process,
the encounters played a shaping role in the self-conscious realization by Europeans that they differed from others in possessing a
unique "civilization."

5

I have noted the presence on Cook's second voyage of two natu-
ralist-anthropologists accompanying him, the Forsters, father and
son. Johann Reinhold Forster was a well-traveled savant who had
spent time in England, where he taught alongside of Joseph
Priestley at Worrington Academy, a dissenting school. When Joseph Banks withdrew from the planned second expedition, he
was replaced by Forster as principal naturalist. The latter insisted
that his son, Georg, then eighteen years old, come too. Both father and son produced their own accounts of the voyage, the
former publishing a *Journal* and *Observations Made During a
Voyage Round the World* (1778), and the latter a *Voyage Round the
World* (1777). It is young Georg's account that is of particular
interest for our purposes.

What we see in his *Voyage* and later writings is that the concept of civilization serves two major purposes. It is first a way of
thinking about the "other," allowing one to define each party as
having or not having a civilization. It is easy to make the distinction. Describing the clearing by Cook's men of some woods at
Dusky Bay in New Zealand, Forster points out that more was

done in a day than the natives, with their tools of stone, could
have done in three months. "The superiority of a state of civilization over that of barbarism could not be more clearly stated, than
by the alterations and improvements we had made in this place,"
he concludes.[21] He goes on to speak of the "advantages, the
blessings which civilization and revealed religion have diffused
over our part of the globe," that is, Europe. At another place, he
comments on the superiority of the "rule of law," which replaces
the violence of savages, and attributes it to agriculture, which
brings "opulence, luxury, and civilization."[22] Material improvement, religion, peace—these, as we have noted with Mirabeau,
are the alleged hallmarks of civilization.

Forster's confident tone can mislead us. In fact, he is extremely ambivalent about the superiority of civilization over the
natives' way of life. Describing the Tahitians, he ascribes to
them the virtues of simplicity and happiness. After one idyllic
passage, he concludes: "Thus contented with their simple way of
life, and placed in a delightful country, they are free from cares,
and happy in their ignorance." The moral and existential superiority seems to be theirs. They are in a position to teach Europeans about the "social affections"—love, friendship and community.[23] So strongly does Forster feel in this mood that he
wishes intercourse between the Europeans and the natives of the
South Seas to be broken off, "before the corruption of manners
which unhappily characterizes civilized regions, may reach that
innocent race of men, who live here fortunate in their ignorance
and simplicity."

He can say this in spite of his awareness of taboo—so much
for innocence—and the practice of infanticide (which he de-
plores). So, too, even while praising the natives' treatment of
women—a mark of civilization—he acknowledges that they are

not allowed to eat with the men. How can we explain this apparent blindness? The answer seems to lie in Forster's desperate search for an alternative to the evils of civilization, while holding on to its advantages. He tried to discover, as one author puts it, "the true foundations for human happiness and morality," and to do so "through empirical research." Alas, the latter came into conflict with the ideal, and it was the empirical that was frequently cast aside. Yet not completely, for Forster was truly an aspiring anthropologist, trying to ground the ideal in the experience of social reality.

I said above that the concept of civilization serves two purposes. The second is that it allows the European to make sense of the universe. It gives him a moral footing and prescribes manners and modes for the proper conduct of social life. In Forster's case, this provision is tied to a vision of history, as the story of human development. It is a unified vision, where the particular and the general come together convincingly. In a fragment on Indian poetry, "On Local and Universal Culture" (1791), he takes up again the theme I have touched on above and writes: "The local, the specific, the peculiar must melt into the universal, if the prejudices of partiality are to be vanquished. Universality has taken the place of the particular European character, and we are on the way of becoming an idealised people, abstracted from the whole of the human kind, which on account of its knowledge and, may I add, its aesthetic as well as moral perfection, can be styled as the representative of the entire species."[24]

We hear here the sounds of conjectural history, the idea of progress, the treating of the species as a single individual, a single mind—and, mostly, the concept of civilization. It is civilization that embodies the universal, rising above the quotidian details of the particular and other. All can aspire to it, and it can be the

guiding light for all. Europeans are superior, not because of in-
nate qualities, but because they are at the forefront of history. For
Forster, it is not race, for example, that gives the palm to Cook's
voyagers, but improvement; and improvement is attainable by all
peoples. Similarly, although climate may play a favoring role, it is
not decisive in the scale of achievement, as Forster demonstrates
by comparing two tribes in the same general location but with
very different levels of accomplishment.

In sum, Forster shows us that the concept of civilization can
serve as a means to think about and relate to the "other," and also
as a way of making moral and intellectual sense of the universe.
He has taken the observations of Cook's *Voyages* and added to
them both his own observations and philosophical-anthropologi-
cal conjectures. He serves, therefore, as a nice, brief additional
case history in our own study of the phenomenon of civilization
and its contents in the late eighteenth century.

6

In 1793, Lord Macartney led an embassy to China in order to establish settled relations with the Qianlong Emperor. Here, the
encounter, unlike in the South Seas, was with an "other" who
had equivalent claims to being a civilization, equal to or even superior to that of the West. Historians have generally treated
Macartney's embassy as a failure, but closer examination shows it
to have been a meeting of Kipling's East and West, whose outcome was troubled and ambiguous, with Macartney as something of a cosmopolitan hero. His *Journal*, which ends in 1794
(but was not published until much later), becomes a prime text in
the entire story.

Many in the West in the seventeenth and eighteenth centuries
saw China as, in fact, a superior civilization to that of Europe.

That perception was to undergo a great change in the century that followed, a change that should not warp our view of the earlier period. From the time of Marco Polo's travels to the visits of the Jesuits, China was clearly recognized as a very rich, powerful, and advanced part of the world. It was also the most populated country in existence, numbering around 400 million inhabitants in the eighteenth century. Its self-image was that of being the center of the world, the Middle Kingdom.

The word supplied by Chinese scholars as equivalent to "civilization" is *wenming*, but this has a different connotation to the word *civilisation* as employed by Mirabeau and the Europeans who followed him. It refers mainly to the legitimacy of the Chinese sovereigns who had ruled since the time of the mythical sage-kings in accordance with Tian Ming, the Mandate of Heaven. As one author puts it, "'All under Heaven,' variously interpreted as the Empire, China, or the World, was given as a fief to the best man in it, recognized as Tian Zi, the Son of Heaven."[25] He was to rule it as Heaven would have ruled it; and how Heaven would rule was made clear in the works of Confucius and his followers.

Confucian orthodoxy justified the rule of the despotic establishment, under the emperor, at the same time as it established a moral and ideological measuring rod to restrain its excesses. As the possessor of the Mandate of Heaven, China had the right, and often the might, to extract tribute from its neighbors. There was no question of mutual and equal exchange; China was simply the superior. As another author puts it, China was a "civilization with customs, religions, manners, modes of dress, ceremonies, arts, abundant natural resources, a seemingly infinite variety of manufactured goods, and an extensive written history." With this inheritance in mind, the emperor in 1656 addressed the

Dutch, who were seeking trade relations, as follows: "from afar you know and long for our virtue and civilization, and respect and admire Us, your Sovereign and Father."[26]

In the shape of Macartney's embassy, we witness the "clash" of two civilizations. Each challenged the other's self-image. As in 1656 with the Dutch, the emperor addressed the British ambassador in superior terms: "We, by the Grace of Heaven, Emperor, instruct the King of England to take note of our charge. Although your country, O King, lies in the far oceans, yet inclining your heart toward civilization you have specially sent an envoy respectfully to present a state message, and sailing the seas he has come to our Court to kowtow and to present congratulations for the Imperial birthday, and also to present local products, thereby showing your sincerity."[27] Macartney, while he acknowledged the power and wealth of his Chinese hosts, and admired their refinement, was not prepared to admit their superiority. The kowtow became the symbol of this difference in perception. Macartney was willing to kowtow to the emperor if his opposite number in China would kowtow to the British king; alternatively, Macartney was willing to go down on one knee, as he would before his own king.

The symbolic gesture embodied the question of civilization on both sides. For the Chinese emperor, whose claim to legitimacy was based on uniquely having the Mandate of Heaven, the notion of international equality was not conceivable. To admit that he was only one monarch among many, on a par with some obscure king across the seas, was to shake the foundations of his rule to the core. It cut to the very heart of the Chinese version of civilization. Yet for the British envoy to accept the Chinese view of things was to concede inferiority in terms of civilization itself, a Western achievement, and one in fact on the verge of becoming

superior to the Chinese; for such was the actual situation, as revealed by the initial British seizure of Macao a decade later, in
1802.

   In 1793, however, this event was still in the wings. We are on
the edge of the shift to come. The two claimants to "civilization"
were still feeling each other out. In what follows, I explore only
from the European side—the Chinese version would be another
story, to be touched upon in my last chapter—with Macartney as
our guide. He was both aware of Chinese achievements and prepared to praise them. Thus, he wrote of his reception as showing
"that calm dignity, that sober pomp of Asiatic greatness, which
European refinements have not yet attained." He admired Chinese agriculture and its beauty, and considered the Chinese "certainly the best husbandmen in the world." He acknowledged
Chinese prowess in the arts, "particularly in the manufacture of
silk stuffs and of certain kinds of cotton cloth," and conceded
their excellence especially in pottery, that is, the production of
porcelain. He also understood that the Chinese were advanced in
science and technology. In his train, Macartney had brought
globes, clocks, a planetarium as presents for the emperor. As he
himself observes, however, his hosts already had spheres, orreries,
clocks, and "musical automatons of such exquisite workmanship,
and in such profusion, that our presents must shrink from the
comparison."[28]

   What the Chinese didn't have was incipient industrialization,
well under way in Great Britain, along with its latent application
to war. Macartney sensed that, although the Chinese were advanced in scientific and technological understanding, they made
little effective use of their knowledge. Nor were they curious to go
further in this direction. Thus, when Macartney offered to take
some of the Chinese officials up in a hot air balloon that he had

brought with him, they declined the "experiment." They showed little awareness that the balloon was the forerunner, or rather the symbol, of future Western superiority in the area of science and technology, later to be made manifest in the form of the gunboat.

In 1793, however, Macartney assessed Chinese civilization, marked as it was by such traits as agricultural production, stable government, refinement of manners, and so forth, as on the whole equal to that of the West. True, he had reservations even about Chinese refinement, especially in regard to cleanliness. He found even people of first rank uncleanly and given to spitting "about the rooms without mercy." Their table manners were not to his taste—for example, they had no forks—and were "foul . . . eaters of garlic"; and, at the other end, they had no water closets.

But he was also aware of equivalent European lapses. Thus, when lamenting the Chinese custom of foot binding, he remembers that his own countrywomen go in for tight shoes, high heels, and ponderous buckles, not to mention corsets, which are comparable disfigurements. As a civilized man, Macartney was aware that there are certain universals among humans, such as the need to distort and ornament our "natural" shape, to be encountered "from the politest nations of Europe to the most barbarous islanders of the South Seas." "In traveling . . . whenever I meet with anything singular or extraordinary, I usually endeavour to recollect whether I have seen anything analogous to it elsewhere," he tells us, as a kind of cosmopolitan anthropologist. "By comparing such objects together and attentively marking their similitude and difference a common origin of principles, customs and manners may sometimes be traced and discovered in nations the most remote from each other."

Macartney and Forster, to stay with these two, may not have been shipmates, but they were certainly soul mates. They both

sought universal principles that ordered human nature and relations. They did so on both ends of the spectrum of being civilized, Forster voyaging in the South Seas, with its semi-barbarous
native populations, and Macartney traveling in China, with its
advanced civilization. In these disparate mirrors, they sought to
catch the reflection of European civilization—and to reflect on it.
Their version of civilization was a generous one. "The Chinese, it
is true, are a singular people, but they are men formed of the
same materials and governed by the same passions as ourselves,"
Macartney remarked. He understood why they were suspicious of
the Englishmen visiting them, who often acted with arrogance
and contempt for what they themselves, the Englishmen, did not
understand. Macartney was different, however, from most or at
least many of his compatriots. "[N]othing could be more falla-
cious than to judge of China by any European standard," he declared.

Emphasizing a common humanity, empathy, and the acceptance of the difference of the other, Macartney reflected the toler-
ant Enlightenment definition of civilization. It was a form of social relation open to all peoples, and achieved by them in different
ways and in different degrees. It was based on improvement, not
on an essence such as race. Alas, it was racism, however, that
would come increasingly to characterize the European civilization
that, by the first few decades of the nineteenth century, stood in
confrontation to other peoples. At this point, in fact, the concept
of civilization became an obstacle to any real understanding of
the other. Instead, it served as an ideology by which to condemn
and then to control "barbarians," that is, inferiors.

To anticipate a later chapter, we can see just how bad the
situation was to be when we read the words of Lord Palmerston,
in 1850, that "the Time is fast coming when we shall be obliged to

strike another blow in China." Locating it among the "half civilized Governments"—how far we have come from Macartney's
even-handed account—Palmerston advocated the same solution
as required for recalcitrant schoolboys: "[T]hey must not only see
the Stick but actually feel it upon their shoulders."[29] As early as
1802 and 1808, the British had applied the "Stick" in Macao. By
1842 and the Opium War with China, they were laying about
them mightily. Eight years later, Palmerston could announce as
policy what before had only been a spreading practice.

At the heart of this new version of civilization was the notion
of race, as the basis for claims of superiority. The British lord saw
civilization as imposing a "blood" duty on him to rule all others.
A virulent racism had become part of his self-image. Adumbrated
in parts of the cerebral discourses of late eighteenth-century anthropological speculations, racism gained strength from the early
nineteenth-century British experience in India (ousting its utilitarian rival in the process), and from the needs of British imperialism. Shortly, it would receive support from "Social Darwinism." Even before the *Origin of Species* was published in 1859,
however, racism appeared to have scientific underpinnings in, for
example, the writings of such inquirers as Buffon and Linnaeus,
but now especially in J. A. de Gobineau's *Essai sur l'inégalité des
races humaines* (the first part of which was translated in 1915 as
The Inequality of the Races), published in 1853–55—and dedicated
to King George V of Hanover.

We are a long way from Macartney's China as an admired and
equal claimant to civilization; now, as yellow men, the Chinese
were excluded from that level of advancement. Race had become
destiny, and the determinant of civilization. Science had become
ideology, as had the very notion of civilization itself.

7

We have been looking at three episodes in the story of civilization as a concept in the late eighteenth century, treating them as part of its contents. Cook's South Seas voyages and his account thereof, Forster's own account of one of those voyages, and Macartney's journal of his embassy to China have been our prime texts in this, our own attempt at exploration. The first two, dealing with relatively "primitive" societies, were engaged in an effort to understand the "other," partly in his own terms, as a member of a unique group, and partly as serving as an illustration of the universal nature of mankind, expressing itself in different ways. In their work pursuant to this effort, Cook and Forster sought to understand the origins and definition of civilization in religion, property arrangements, marital ways, mores and manners, and so forth. Macartney's encounter, in turn, was with an advanced civilization, but he had similar purposes in mind, along with the simple desire to record impressions as he experienced them.

In all of these cases, the result was a defining, or redefining, of European civilization, as well as of the other. Seeing itself in the mirror of the other, the West could reflect upon itself and its identity. It was a benign reflection in general. Within a few decades, however, a disfigurement occurred in what was seen in the mirror. The other took on the visage of an inferior race, condemned to be half-civilized—and to be ruled by a superior, European civilization. A benign colonial ideology—for even Cook, Forster, and Macartney were carriers in part of this superior and self-serving attitude—was increasingly replaced by a more savage colonial ideology, masquerading as civilization.

3

Civilization as European Ideology

1

In the century following the excursions of Cook, Forster, and Macartney, the discourse of civilization hung in the European air as well as in and about its colonies and intended dependencies. After its coinage in the mid eighteenth century, the concept was invoked as a mantra. It lurks, of course, behind Edward Gibbon, writing in 1776 on the decline and fall of the Roman Empire (although he does not use the word "civilization"), and it is present in Burke's *Reflections on the Revolution in France* of 1790, where he sees the revolutionaries as the new barbarians, attacking "[o]ur manners, our civilization, and all the good things which are connected with manners, and with civilization."[1] Earlier, in 1772, Dr. Johnson had refused to admit the word into his *Dictionary* in its fourth edition. The faithful Boswell tells us why: "He would not admit *civilization*, but only *civility*. With great deference to him, I thought *civilization*, from *to civilize*, better in the sense opposed to *barbarity*, than *civility*."[2]

As so often, Johnson was fighting a losing battle. The chatter of civilization swept over him not only in his own century but even more so in the nineteenth century. No future dictionary could avoid the word. It figures in the title of innumerable works and can be found in the contents of even more. Invoked in many situations, it was especially used to define Europe as the model of civilization, in comparison to other places, and, increasingly in this effort, given a racist tone to set the favored peoples off from the lesser breeds. Among the many works and authors that could serve to illustrate this development, I shall choose three. They are in many ways prototypic of what I am treating as a European ideology.

My three are François Guizot and his *Histoire générale de la civilisation en Europe* (followed quickly by *Histoire de la civilisation en France*); Arthur de Gobineau and his *Essai sur l'inégalité des races humaines* (which, although it does not have the word "civilization" in its title, has it in many of its chapter headings); and, perhaps to some rather surprisingly in this context, Charles Darwin, especially in regard to his *Voyage of the Beagle* and *Descent of Man*. I could also, or in place of these three, have examined such figures and works as Henry Thomas Buckle and his *History of Civilization in England* (1857), or Matthew Arnold and his *Culture and Anarchy* (1869); or turned, for example, to various German, Italian, or Spanish authors, to stay only within the European context.

I have chosen Guizot because his was an early and highly influential attempt to define the content of European civilization and, in a benign tone (thus continuing that of our authors of the previous chapter), to analyze the grounds for its superiority over others; Gobineau because his has become a classic statement (irrespective of its literary or scholarly merits, of which it has few or none), both in his time and ours, of the racist argument for that superiority; and Darwin because in the most subtle and pervasive manner his wonderful achievement in regard to evolutionary theory carried with it racist undertones (sometimes overt tones) that entered into the whole of European culture and its discourse of civilization.

2

In 1827, François Guizot began a series of lectures in the Sorbonne, which were published a year later as *The History of Civilization in Europe* (to give it its English translation). The theme was highly political, for these were the last years of the Restoration, and Guizot's lectures held up a mirror for his own compatriots, as well as for the rest of the world. Indeed, his usage reminds us that discussions of civilization are always about current events as much as about scholarly inquiry (we have already noted this in the case of Mirabeau, and, logically, it must apply to the present book). In fact, the revolution that followed in 1830 removed Charles X from power and brought in the so-called bourgeois monarchy of Louis-Philippe. One of those who served him, becoming chief minister in 1840 and remaining in that post until the overthrow of the July Monarchy in 1848, and its replacement by the Second Republic, was our author. Thus, Guizot's lectures were a springboard of sorts to his active involvement in political life, an involvement that in the end discredited him—for he was ultimately seen as a lackey of middle-class interests. Subsequently, his contributions as a historian were obscured.

It is as historian and discussant about civilization, however, that we are interested in the erstwhile minister, while not overlooking the political context in which he lived. To return to his lectures of 1827, Guizot was proposing a system of representative government as offering the possibility of reform instead of revolution to the France of his day. But more than this, he was placing his recommendations in a broad philosophical and historical framework—actually a form of philosophy of history—that sought to analyze the nature of Europe and its institutions and to distinguish it and them from others. It is this part of his work that has lasted beyond the immediate political circumstances of his composition. It is primarily for this reason that, for example, Tocqueville sat in the audience and subsequently introduced Guizot's inspiration into the writing of his *Democracy in America*, and why John Stuart Mill wrote favorable reviews of the author of the *History of Civilization*.

What did they hear and read? What Guizot told them was that civilization was a "fact": "susceptible, like any other, of being studied, described, narrated."[3] There is a "positive" sound to this initial assertion. In fact, the father of positivism, Auguste Comte was to begin his Paris lectures on the *Cours de philosophie positif* a few years later, in 1832; his conception of social facts—sociology—was thus anticipated in principle in one part by his compatriot. Guizot, for his part, added that he was dealing with a "general, hidden, complex fact."

People ask, is civilization good or evil? Guizot answers that he is "convinced that there is, in reality, a general destiny of humanity, a transmission of the aggregate of civilization; and consequently, an universal history of civilization to be written. . . . this history is the greatest of all, that it includes all."[4] This is not, however, the history that Guizot undertakes to write. His account is to be restricted to Europe. Yet the vision of a single history of civilization lingers over his account, implicit in the idea of progress and its providential nature.

In Guizot's words, "The idea of progress, of development, appears to me the fundamental idea contained in the word, *civilization*." Appealing to the etymology of the word, Guizot identifies its meaning as "the perfecting of civil life, the development of society, properly so called, of the relations of men among themselves."[5] Where do we find this development in its highest form? It is in Europe, and, as we shall see, in France especially. The defining mark of European civilization is its pluralism, for no one value or institution, unlike in other civilizations—Egyptian, for example—has prevailed over time.

In its history, European civilization has drawn upon three major sources. The first is Rome, with its heritage of municipal institutions, self-government, and the idea of the state as sovereign power. The second is Christianity, with its idea that the moral law is superior to legislative law, and with its attendant separation of spiritual and temporal powers. The third is, in essence, feudalism, with its overcoming of the barbarism that succeeded the end of Roman power, and its establishment of a "German" idea of liberty and individuality. The vicissitudes of these three elements and their intermixing, into whose details Guizot enters (we shall not), assured the diversity that distinguishes European from all other civilizations. Also from this pluralism and diversity emerges the fact of classes with their own interests and values, whose competition ensures that Europe will not remain stationary as is the case elsewhere (e.g., Egypt, India, and even Greece).

Seemingly echoing Mirabeau's dictum, Guizot announces that "[a]t all times, in all countries, religion has assumed the glory of having civilized the people."[6] Only then is it joined in this task by sciences, letters, and the arts. It is obviously only the Christian religion, however, that leads on to further development toward the optimum in civilized social existence. Islam is faulted, for example, because of its combination of the spiritual and temporal powers, which leads to tyranny, as well as to the "stationary condition into which that civilization is everywhere fallen." In contrast, "European civilization," as Guizot enlightens us, "has en-

tered, if we may so speak, into the eternal truth, into the plan of
Providence; it progresses according to the intentions of God. This
is the rational account of its superiority."[7]

At the forefront of God's intentions, happily, is France. Its peculiar characteristics are "perspicuity, sociability, sympathy."[8]
Our general good sense, looking at France from the seventeenth
century on, assures us that it was and is "the most civilized country in Europe." Europe as the foremost civilization, France as its
most civilized country: these are providential facts. Providence, as
we know, is a Christian notion. Even in the secular eighteenth
century, it was taken for granted. Adam Smith invoked it directly
in defense of capitalism, as well as in the form of the invisible
hand (incidentally, capitalism is not mentioned by Guizot in his
account, although possibly implicit in his featuring private property as "European"; the "rise" of the bourgeoisie, however, hovers
in the air). Tocqueville, Guizot's "student," was to view the in-
evitable triumph of democracy in America and elsewhere as a
"providential fact."

Without going into further details, we can see how Guizot has
asserted the providential, and therefore not to be questioned, supremacy of European civilization. In more pedestrian terms, he
analyzed the factors, spiritual and material, that entered into that
supremacy. In his most general terms, he agreed that "[c]iviliza-
tion seemed to me to consist of two principal facts: the development of human society, and that of man himself; on the one
hand, political and social development; on the other, internal and
moral development."[9] So stated, civilization was open-ended and
available to other than European peoples.

This opening, however, was effectively closed by Guizot's
definition of religion as the basis of civilization; and the Christian
religion as defining Europe in its most essential sense; and Eu-

rope as God's chosen vessel. Karl Marx may have been partially inspired by Guizot's account to explore further the political, social, and, especially, economic development of Europe and then its expansion out into the world market and world history. Guizot, although having dropped the tantalizing hint of a general civilization to come, contented himself with the European story. In rather plodding prose, bolstered by his providential faith (which echoed his Protestant belief in predestination), Guizot offered an ideological defense of European supremacy as a civilization that, in its low-keyed way, was to become the prevailing gospel of the nineteenth century. The Christian religion had donned secular garb.

3

As is so often the case, there is a line –the famous "six degrees of separation"—leading from Guizot to Gobineau. It runs through Tocqueville, student of one and friend of the other. In 1843, a correspondence between Tocqueville and Gobineau started, with the former seeking to enlist Gobineau's aid in writing a work on European moral and social habits. The two may have met briefly a few years earlier, but, in any case, Tocqueville had read and been impressed by an article on Greece written in 1841 by the younger man. The resulting epistolary exchange offers a wonderful glimpse into the two minds and their thoughts about civilization.

A central issue is religion and morality. Tocqueville argues that although modern society may be antitheological, it is not anti-Christian; nor should it be, for Christianity, admittedly neglecting public virtue, nevertheless serves as the inspiration and justification for the promotion of equality. Gobineau takes an opposite position, claiming that Christianity is basically inter-

ested only in personal salvation. Thus, a new morality has become necessary. It is to be one "brought down to earth," that is, a
secularized creed. As we can see, this new morality is suspiciously
close to what will later be advocated by Nietzsche, who admits to
having read the *Essai*.

In the correspondence, Tocqueville confesses to being "greatly
prejudiced against what seems to be your principal idea, which
. . . seems to belong to a group of materialistic theories." He
continues: "You continually speak about races regenerating or
degenerating . . . to me, this sort of predestination [Tocqueville
should have blushed at this charge, given his own proclivity to
the idea] is a close relative of the purest materialism." In a final
burst of exasperation, Tocqueville demands, "Don't you see how
inherent in your doctrine are all the evils produced by permanent
inequality . . . ?"[10]

His friend saw full well. In fact, racism for Gobineau was a
defense of, and an explanation for, inequality. If a materialist, as
Tocqueville labeled him, he was nevertheless not a Marxist materialist, pressing on to the fullest equality. Quite the opposite. His
materialism was, he claimed, grounded in science, which established with certainty that humanity was necessarily and always in
a condition of inequality. As he wrote Tocqueville, "the methods
I have chosen are exclusively scientific . . . obviously independent
of the consent of the majority." Then he added, "I am mathe-
matically certain about the correctitude of my propositions."[11]

In *Democracy in America*, Tocqueville thought that he had
discovered not only a new world but a "new political science," by
which in fact he meant historical sociology. At first glance,
Gobineau's racial science might be far removed from the spirit of
his friend's attempt. In fact, it was also a historical sociological
reading of history, accounting for the past and the present state of

humanity and its civilizations. In one case, the reading is under the sign of free will (although we have noted the providential element in Tocqueville), liberty, and democracy. In the other case, under the sign of determinism (hence the charge of materialism), inherited traits, and permanent inequality.

Before leaving the two men and their correspondence, and turning directly to the *Essai* and its author, we ought to satisfy our curiosity as to how, given such different opinions, they were able to remain friends. The fact is that, aside from a father-son element, the two men came from similar royalist backgrounds and had overlapping scholarly and political interests. The difference is that Tocqueville resignedly accepted the French Revolution and the coming of democracy; his friend did not, thereby perhaps echoing a repressed sentiment in the soul of the other. An alternative explanation, for those alienated by the language of repression, is that differences attract, especially where there are underlying similarities.[12]

4

Gobineau's early life was marked by unhappy family circumstances—both parents living beyond their means, enveloped in legitimist illusions, engaging in adulterous relations, and filling the young boy's head with claims of royal descent. If one takes seriously Nietzsche's comment that philosophy is the confession of the philosopher, one might interpret Gobineau's racist theories as in part a redemption of his aristocratic forebears, now fallen on degenerate circumstances. In any case, there were other features of Gobineau's life that bore more overtly on his future work. After rattling around in various clerical jobs, he was introduced to Tocqueville in one of the royalist salons. Tocqueville, impressed with the young man's interest in literature and gift for foreign

languages, secured him a position in the foreign ministry. Another royalist friend secured for him the post of first secretary in
Bern, from where he went on to serve in Hanover and Frankfurt.
Gobineau had a gift for languages, and this served him well.
He held posts in Persia, Greece, Brazil, and Sweden between 1854
and 1877. Along the way, he met Bismarck (whom he disliked),
Emperor Dom Pedro of Brazil, and Richard Wagner. He was, in
fact, a successful diplomat, writing various books about his experiences and the countries to which he had been posted. A *Histoire
des Perses* took its place next to his *Trois ans en Asie*. In the latter
book, published four years after the *Essai*, he wrote: "I attempted
to reject every idea of superiority, whether true or false, concerning the peoples whom I have been studying. I wished to assume,
as much as possible, their different points of view, before pro-
nouncing a judgment on their manner of being or feeling" ("J'ai
taché de repudier toute idée vraie ou fausse de superiorité sur les
peuples que j'étudiais. J'ai voulu me placer autant que possible à
leurs différents points de vue, avant de prononcer un jugement
sur leurs façons d'être ou de sentir").[13] Forster could not have put
it better. Yet this is the same Gobineau who four years earlier had
penned his *Essai*, one of the most influential statements proclaiming one-sided racial theories ever written.

The fact is that Gobineau's life and thoughts, aside from the
Essai, were far more complex and even attractive than the theories
advanced in his book. Yet it is the book that persists in European
culture, a landmark of sorts. Why its persistence? The ideas advanced there are puerile, poorly argued, and frequently contradictory. The answer is that Gobineau gave voice to a strong, even
if somewhat incoherent, strain in the threnody of the Europe of
his time and thereafter. He spoke of civilization and its decline at
a time of heightened fears in Europe and offered a powerful ex-

planation of how such degeneration occurred. The simple answer was race. In one all-encompassing doctrine, Gobineau explained that racial developments accounted for the rise and fall of various groups of people and that the meaning of history resides solely in this rise and fall and the domination and subordination of certain races to others.

In the dedication of his *Essai* to George V of Hanover, Gobineau declared that in this time of bloody wars and revolution, he had discovered "the hidden causes of these terrible upheavals" and "the master key to the enigma" of history.[14] He had gradually realized, he says, that "the racial question over-shadows all other problems of history" and "holds the key to them all." The rest of the book is about the application of this key to civilizations and their rise and fall. While the birth, he declares, is fairly simple and obvious, "the fall of civilizations is the most striking, and, at the same time, the most obscure of all the phenomena of history."

What follows this opening sentence is a pastiche of assertions, pseudoscientific statements, and "theories," but the basic theme shines through clearly. Civilizations are based on the accomplishments of a pure race (even this view is, however, muddied). Over time, the race degenerates through a mixing of blood, and thus declines. Gobineau's views on race draw upon the earlier eighteenth-century arguments about the mono- or polygenesis of the human species (such names as Kames and Buffon figure, to which can be added Blumenthal and Cuvier) and on the supposed classification by biologists and anthropologists of mankind into the white, black, and yellow races. This is the "science" of which he was thinking when he wrote to Tocqueville about the scientific status of the *Essai*. To Gobineau's mind, although Providence, that is, "the finger of God in the conduct of the

world," is the ultimate cause (Gobineau, incidentally, was a
nominal Catholic), it is in the "laws which . . . govern organic
and inorganic nature alike" that we must seek our explanations.[15]

Almost at random, I shall select certain of Gobineau's an-
nouncements. For example, he makes much of blood. There is a
natural repugnance, he tells us, to a crossing of blood. Degeneration takes place when there is no longer the same blood running
in the veins of the original conquering race. There is a "ladder of
civilization," and the African races occupy the bottom rung, with
the yellow just above them; and nothing can change this biologi-
cally based inferiority. Climate and soil, he declares, have nothing
to do with civilization. The "lesson of history," he informs us is
that "all civilizations derive from the white race," and "none can
exist without its help."[16] Here we have a direct statement of the
Aryan thesis; yet surprisingly, perhaps, Gobineau has high praise
for the Jewish "race" (who are, of course, white).

Against Guizot, he argues that civilization is not an event—a
"serious error" of Guizot's *Histoire générale*—but "a series, a
chain of events linked more or less logically together and brought
about by the inter-action of ideas which are themselves often very
complex."[17] Joining argument with scientists such as Camper,
Blumenbach, and Owen, Gobineau pretends to be their equal,
offering learned footnotes. He also cites Lyell, but he seems not to
have taken to heart the latter's long geological time, instead af-
firming that the earth has only existed for about 7,000 years. By
such means, and by his wide-ranging references to other civilizations—although he does not allow Christianity to figure as
one—Gobineau festoons his work with the flowers of science.

It is more fitting to see the *Essai* as a work of ideology. As
Gobineau himself acknowledged, his was a contribution to
"moral genealogy." As biology and history tell us, he claims,

some are born to rule and others to serve. Compassion and the softer virtues have no place in Gobineau's morality. In a later work, *La Renaissance*, Gobineau has Cesare Borgia justify to his sister the strangling of her husband by saying, "This is not a monster, my lass, but a dominator . . . for this kind of person whom destiny calls to dominate over others, the ordinary rules of life are reversed and duty becomes completely different" ("Ce n'est pas un monstre, ma fille, c'est un dominateur . . . pour ces sortes de personnes que la destinée appelle à dominer sur les autres, les règles ordinaires de la vie se renversent et le devoir devient tout différent"). As he concludes approvingly, the great law of the world "is to live, to grow greater, and to develop" ("c'est de vivre, de grandir et de développer").[18] We are, it seems, in the dark world of Dostoevsky, only with a pronounced racist message. It remained only to place the emphasis, not on superior individuals, but on superior groups, that is, races, to justify the European right to rule.

5

At a time when Europeans were troubled and anxious over the fast-changing societies in which they were living, the notion of a fixed and presumably stable identity, such as race, was alluring. It could be buttressed by appeals both to religion and to science. With the secular gathering strength in the nineteenth century, the phrases of science seemed more powerful. Indeed, Gobineau and his followers sought to define Europe as no longer being equivalent to Christianity—after all, others could also be Christians—and to cast its identity as a matter of race. Difficult as it might be to establish a solid definition of race, the average person could tell the difference between colors; or so it seemed.

In fact, race is what today we call a social construct. As much as nationalism, it was and is an imagined "community." We take it for granted, even though the word does not appear, for example, in the original language of the Bible and cannot be found in the Greek historians. Indeed, the concept appears to emerge only around the seventeenth century. In a sense, one can argue that race is a product of "modernity" and a partial response to it. It arose in contradistinction to the latter's attack on traditional structures of authority, a revolt that took on the form of claims to equality and democracy. Racial distinctions could replace the faltering aristocratic ones as a justification for hierarchy.

With the advent of the concept of civilization in the eighteenth century, race could find a host on which to fasten itself. Conjectural history, with its stages of development from savages and barbarians, via nomads and agriculturalists, to commercialists and civilization, supplied the general model. Now race became the master key by which to turn that lock of history. By the mid nineteenth century, it could link to work being done in fields such as phrenology and linguistics, as well as to biology, as noted before. It could play effectively on the anxieties about degeneration both of body and soul, individual and society, that were becoming increasingly widespread.

European civilization by the nineteenth century also meant increased division of labor—and classes. It meant workers in trade unions locked in struggle with capitalists. In describing this intestinal conflict within civilization, the ideology of racism was handy for those who saw themselves as the defenders of civilization against the internal barbarians. Thus, Burke, Taine, and many others saw the radicalized laborers as "savages," of a different race from civilized men. The same descriptions were applied to criminals and prostitutes, and any others seen as insider threats to European civilization.

Foremost among those who fostered the racial/class ideology, thus extending Gobineau's ideas, was Gustave Le Bon. In his work on crowds, he made the extension from workers to savages very clear, asserting that "[b]y the mere fact that he becomes part of an organized crowd, a man descends several rungs on the ladder of civilization."[19] In short, civilization was threatened by its own barbarians within, and was a fragile veneer, easily shaken off. (Later, we shall see the effect of this view on Freud.) For Le Bon and his followers, at the heart of the struggle over civilization was race. "One can award a Negro a bachelor of arts degree, a doctorate, one cannot make him civilized," was a typical comment by Le Bon. As with Gobineau, Le Bon claimed his theories were confirmed by his travels in other climes and his reading; for his part, he wrote such books as *Civilisation des arabes* (1883), *Civilisation de l'Inde* (1886), and *Les Premiers civilisations* (1889).

Civilizations, races, crowds, masses, these were the muddled elements of nineteenth-century discourse and theory. Powerful anxieties lurked in back of the use of each of these terms. Psychologic may be more useful than logic in explaining their conjunctions as found in some of the writers we have touched on above. In any case, Gobineau's *Essai*, which remains the center of our interest in this section, was one of the earlier and most influential statements showing the affinity of the terms "civilization" and "race." Henceforth, the supremacy of European civilization, as it defined itself against its own inner barbarians, but especially as it sought to subordinate to its rule the rest of the world—lesser peoples and civilizations—carried a simple explanation: racial superiority.[20] The "scientific" explanation, of course, was also a justification, as well as a prescription to cure any possible feelings of guilt.

6

The same muddled elements of European culture that stood in back of Gobineau formed the context in which Darwin did his work. Imperialism, especially in its British mode, was another crucial element. The collections of flora and fauna that served as the basis for Darwin's theorizing were essential to him, and without European explorations and expeditions, these would not have become available. The very voyage of the *Beagle* that gave Darwin firsthand exposure to the globe and its resources was commissioned by the British Admiralty to chart coastal areas for the safety of British ships. Such imperialistic initiatives represented the advance of civilization, certainly in the eyes of the Europeans.

Having said this about imperialism and Darwin, I must also make it clear that we should avoid the etiological fallacy. The theory of evolution by means of natural selection must be judged on its own scientific merits, not on its origins in an imperialistic culture. The same can be said about Darwin's connection to nineteenth-century capitalism. He was tied into it, not only directly through his Wedgwood grandparent, but by his upper-middle-class status and education. This capitalist society and its prevalent views could hardly be escaped by Darwin, except perhaps in a few particulars. Competition was not only in the "economy of nature" but in the society in which Darwin came upon his evolutionary theories. Again, however, the etiological fallacy must be avoided in regard to his theories about evolution.

It should not be surprising that much of Darwin's work is concerned with the questions of civilization and race. Perhaps it is the exceptional importance of *The Origin of Species*, setting forth his general theory, and which is not concerned with humans and their evolutionary development, that may lead us to

overlook his otherwise topical concerns. These manifest themselves, for example, both in his early work *The Voyage of the Beagle* and his later *The Descent of Man* and need greater acknowl-
edgment than they are usually given. It is no demeaning of Darwin, for whom I have the greatest admiration, to say that his
mind is frequently mired in the clay of his own times. As a
"philosophical naturalist" (his own term), he sought to apply his
scientific method of observation and theorizing to the understanding of humans and their cultural evolution, as much as their
physical evolution. Again not surprisingly, the results are vastly
different as to their scientific standing from his work on the origin of species.

7

Darwin's initial encounter with uncivilized beings, which made
him reflect insistently on the subject at large, was in the shape of
the Fuegians. The encounter seems almost traumatic, and its
memory is recalled in a number of places. Typical is Darwin's account in the *Voyage of the Beagle* of his first meeting with some of
the inhabitants of Tierra del Fuego at the tip of South America.
"It was," he tells us, "without exception the most curious and
interesting spectacle I ever beheld: I could not have believed how
wide was the difference between savage and civilized man: it is
greater than between a wild and domesticated animal, inasmuch
as in man there is a greater power of achievement."[21]

These particular Fuegians were tall and possessed of some
primitive garments. The next group Darwin encountered were
naked and small. "These poor wretches were stunted in their
growth, their hideous faces bedaubed with white paint, their
skins filthy and greasy, their hair entangled, their voices discor-

dant, and their gestures violent," he writes. "Viewing such men, one can hardly make oneself believe that they are fellow-creatures, and inhabitants of the same world."[22] The gulf between the white man and the "other," separating the cultivated Englishman and the "barbarians," as he calls them, has opened wide.

In fact, Darwin had already met Fuegians earlier. On an earlier voyage, Robert FitzRoy, the captain of the *Beagle*, had "captured" three members of the tribe and brought them back to London. Here, they were viewed as curios, given English names—Jemmy Button, York Minster (named after a mountain discovered by Captain Cook), and Fuegia Basket—and exposed to Christianity and a modest education. Now, in 1831, they were being returned to their native land on board the *Beagle*. Like animals once tainted in captivity by contact with humans, these three Fuegians were not welcomed back by their brethren, who promptly stripped them of their Western finery. In any event, knowing them had obviously not prepared Darwin for the habitat from which they had come, in which the Fuegians were in the wild. Hence the more or less traumatic encounter. As he repeated toward the end of his *Descent of Man*, "The astonishment which I felt on seeing a party of Fuegians on a wild and broken shore will never be forgotten by me."[23]

That astonishment, I want to maintain, helped transform Darwin into an unconscious racist of sorts (adding to the baggage he brought with him from home). He labels these "fellow-creatures" childlike; and worse, compares them to orangutans (perhaps inspired to this comparison by a classification supplied earlier by Linnaeus).[24] At another place he uses the word "cannibal." He is repulsed by their treatment of women and notices their lack of religion as a civilizing force. The poles of his thought are civilization and barbarism. In noticing the Fuegians' lack of the former, he defines the conditions for it more or less by default. As he remarks, "The perfect equality among the individuals composing the Fuegian tribes, must for a long time retard their civilization." Other essentials of civilization are property, a fixed abode, ranks, and a chief.

The Fuegians are on the lowest rung of civilization, if even allowed to be there. Other tribes and groups encountered by Darwin on the voyage are constantly being placed on the ladder. Even the Esquimaux rank higher than the Fuegians, he informs us, and "[t]he South Sea Islanders of the two races inhabiting the Pacific, are comparatively civilized."[25] Wherever he journeys on his voyage, he takes with him the measuring rod of civilization. Not for nothing had Darwin read his Gibbon and, as he tells us in his *Autobiography*, Buckle's *History of Civilization*, read not once but twice.[26]

The Voyage of the Beagle led to the *Origin of Species*, that momentous breakthrough to evolutionary theory. In this book, as I have suggested, only echoes of the civilization discourse are to be heard, as when Darwin emphasizes that extermination of species is part of nature and an integral balance to their origin. If all species face extinction, then man, too, and all his achievements are also subject to this law. But this is not a theme Darwin overtly develops in the *Origin*. Only in the *Descent* does he revert to topics broached in the *Voyage*, with civilization once more front and center as a theme. This time, again, it is intimately linked to racial as well as evolutionary theory.

It is all too often forgotten that one of the three principal aims of the *Descent* was to consider "the value of the differences between the so-called races of man" (the other two are "whether man, like every other species, is descended from some pre-existing form; secondly, the manner of his development").[27] Critical in our reading of the great naturalist is to note his words "so-called." Classification of various sorts was central to Darwin's thinking, and he was astute enough to recognize that, as with species, races were only with difficulty sharply separated. Nevertheless, the *Descent* is sprinkled with such pejorative terms as "lower races" and "inferior" races.

The whole discussion of what others have called man's ascent is situated in a general discourse about civilization. Thus, an entire chapter is devoted to "The Development of the Intellectual and Moral Faculties During Primeval and Civilised Times." The thread running throughout is the idea of progress. As Darwin comments, it is a Western notion, lacking, for example, among Orientals. Darwin's emphasis is, however, on moral rather than material progress. It is a sense of morality, for example, that allows one tribe to unite and exercise superiority over another. Patriotism, obedience, courage, sympathy, and a willingness "to sacrifice themselves for the common good" make for victory "over most other tribes; and this would be natural selection."[28] (So much for those who see unmitigated competition and self-interest as being Darwin's message; the *Descent* is one long homage to altruism.) It is the Europeans who have been most "moral," and therefore successful in the race of life, if I can so put it.

In the *Descent*, Darwin mixes remarks about breeding with his observations on civilization and race. The elimination of those weak in mind or body improves the race. As we know from other sources, he approved of his cousin Francis Galton's new science of eugenics. Nevertheless, Charles Darwin believed that morality leads members of a group to preserve even those who are weak, and that in a complicated way, this forms part of progress (Darwin himself, incidentally, abominated slavery). The implicit conflict of views simply lingers over the whole of the *Descent* and is never satisfactorily resolved.

Like the Bible, alas, Darwin can be read on both sides of the issues. His, unlike Gobineau's, is a complicated story. My own reading is that the main thrust of Darwin's mind was nonracist, but that he was a victim of his time and culture. His observations on "natural history" showed him that everywhere there were dominant and subordinate members of a species, that the survival of one individual or group was at the expense of another. When he carried over this observation to humans, he unfortunately on occasion attached to it terms such as "inferior." In a rather startling passage, he repeats without judgment the observation of a Mr. Greg that the "'[t]he careless, squalid, unaspiring Irishman' is an 'inferior and *less* favoured race' compared to the 'frugal, foreseeing, self-respecting, ambitious Scot.'"[29] It is clear which one will gain the upper hand. The Irishman and the Fuegian seem to have moved into a composite portrait.

Darwin recognized that all civilized nations had once been barbarous. That once civilized, they could also fall from that estate. Nevertheless, he believed that there was more progress than regression. The historical record seemed to show that that progress was furthest advanced in the European nations and peoples. In this sense they were "fitter" than other "so-called races." Equating progress with morality meant an untroubled conscience. Still, we are startled to hear Darwin at one point exult that at some point not too far in the future the Europeans would beat the Turks hollow![30]

What Darwin illustrates—and I am only trying to portray him as "human, all too human," and not as a fallen idol—is that racism in connection with the concept of civilization was an all-pervasive feature of the nineteenth century in Europe. Unfortunately, there was that in Darwin's own thinking and writing that could give sustenance to the belief in European supremacy. His own conscious and unconscious racist statements could enter into the atmosphere from which they emerged and give it a scientific coloring. It was a different sort of science from that of Gobineau—much more admirable and "progressive"—but none the less equally open to misuse and perversion. That too, along with the glory and the grandeur of evolutionary theory, is part of the legacy of the Darwinian Revolution.

8

My account of what I am calling "a European ideology," by which I mean a racial interpretation of civilization in favor of Europe, has been tied to three figures. They are like markers on a map, allowing for the triangulation of a thesis. While my treatment has been impressionistic, and others could have figured in the account, it allows us to position the various arguments that could underlie the claim to superiority. In their persons, they symbolize a belief system made up of interrelated parts.

Confidence in the unquestioned nature of European civilizational supremacy is the hallmark of Guizot's *History of Civilization*. Emphasizing religion in a secular dress, he enlists both Providence and progress as vital elements in that preeminence. This allows him to speak of Europe, not Christianity (although it is a requisite feature of Europe), as the civilization in question. Although pluralism and diversity set Europe off from other civilizations, these beliefs and attributes, along with a penchant for free institutions, give it a unity. In principle, other peoples might enter into a similar shape of civilization—possibly approximating France, which embodies the highest manifestation of Europe's genius. In practice, it is clear that such emulation can never be successful, for reasons of history and institutionalization that are unique to the West.

What is implicit in Guizot—his confident sense of inimitable superiority—is made manifest in Gobineau and given a new principle: race. Grounding his ideas in biology and "scientific" law, Gobineau makes it clear that race is the distinguishing force behind all of history. With an emphasis on blood, and the identification of purity and power with the white race, in opposition to the black and yellow, Gobineau claimed to have laid down a new "moral genealogy." Girded about by this new morality, European civilization henceforth could go forth and conquer other, lesser peoples and civilizations in the name of a law of nature, without having to resort to Guizot or Tocqueville's Providence.

Darwin was a real scientist. Unlike Gobineau, he engaged in a sober effort to understand human development in the light of evolutionary theory. Nevertheless, as a result of some of that theory's possible implications in regard to struggle and to breeding, as well as his own inheritance from the culture of nineteenth-century Britain, Darwin inadvertently gave support and sustenance to the virulent strain of racism of his time. Educated Europeans could now glory in their civilizational supremacy, thinking that it was justified by the tenets of Social Darwinism (which was, in fact, the theory of Herbert Spencer) as well as Darwinism itself.

The overall result of the kind of work and thinking engaged in by our three representative figures was to turn the benign colonial ideology of men such as Captain Cook, Forster, and Macartney increasingly into a venomous European ideology of supremacy based on a fixed essence: race. The gates of civilization, therefore, or at least of the civilization that counted, that is, the Western model, closed tight in the face of the barbarians without. The division between civilization and barbarism was thus perpetuated in new form, one taken for granted by most Europeans. The only way to eliminate the barbarism of the "others" now would be for them to be swept aside in the name of European civilization, a possession only possible for Europeans.

4

The Civilizing Process

1

In the preceding chapter, we were exposed to a more or less un-
critical account of civilization, coupled with various explanations
of what characterized it and on what it was based. In the present
chapter, I wish to look at more skeptical inquiries into the nature
of civilization and its values. Here the attention will be less on the
reified concept of civilization itself and more on the civilizing
process and its workings (although the line between the two is
hardly rigid). Again, I shall proceed by looking at three figures
and their work, as representing possible approaches to the question of process. My choices—which if somewhat idiosyncratic are
by no mean erratic—are John Stuart Mill, Sigmund Freud, and
Norbert Elias.

2

John Stuart Mill is famous as a preeminent nineteenth-century
British philosopher, economist, and liberal, of a utilitarian bent.
Close examination shows us a complex figure, disposed by char-
acter and his liberal convictions to consider all sides of a question.
As we shall see, this tendency plays out in regard to the topic of

civilization, with one result being that Mill questions its value. His questioning, in turn, is situated in an effort to understand the civilizing process itself.

It should not surprise us that once again we find personal connections among our chosen thinkers on the subject: they are engaged in a common European discourse. Mill, like Gobineau, was a friend of Tocqueville's, and he reviewed the latter's *Democracy in America* and had extensive correspondence with him. Subsequently, there is a connection with Freud. As a twenty-four-year-old student, and short of money, Freud agreed to translate four of Mill's essays for a collected edition of his work in German edited by Theodore Gomperz. The essays included one on the "Enfranchisement of Women" and another on "Socialism." Thus, we know that Freud read Mill; we do not know, however, whether he read Mill's essay on "Civilization" or his comments on that subject in the corpus of his writings. We can only speculate.

Mill's essay on "Civilization" (1836) needs to be considered in conjunction with his essays on Bentham (1838) and Coleridge (1840), whom he treated as "opposite poles of one great force of progression."[1] Without going into any detail, I think we can recognize that Mill, after he reached adulthood, always swung between these two poles. This is already recognizably the case in his 1836 essay.

According to Mill, civilization has a double meaning. It stands (1) for human improvement in general, and (2) for certain kinds of improvement, namely, those that establish the difference between civilized peoples and "savages and barbarians." The first sort of improvement results from the civilizing process over extended time; the second is more recent—as Mill comments, "The present era is preeminently the era of civilization, in the narrow sense"—and is accompanied by vices as well as virtues.[2]

Mill's treatment of the savage seems to me a parody, in which he shows himself totally ignorant of anthropological knowledge. In contrast, he portrays Great Britain as the most civilized force in the nineteenth century. Britain draws strength from its adherence to property and to powers of mind, and from the growth of the middle class. Owing, moreover, to what he identifies as the natural laws of the progress of wealth, Britain has increased the possibility of connections—Mill instances newspapers and the railroad—and multiplied its population. One aspect of the latter is the coming of the masses. And here Mill sees the potential vice of civilization of his second sort: the dominance of public opinion by an uneducated mass and an effeminate, puffed-up upper class. With a diatribe about Oxbridge, the university system, Mill ends by calling for the weak side of civilization to be strengthened by higher cultivation, in the spirit of Coleridge (and reminding us of Matthew Arnold).

The essay does not appear to me one of Mill's stronger pieces. It is too mixed an argument about an abstraction and the politics of the time. Its main importance may well be that it is yet another tribute to the omnipresence of the topic of civilization. We need to go elsewhere in Mill's work to see what he really means by his tergiversation on the subject. His further ruminations, as we shall see, are not much, but they are important for the attention they pay to the way in which civilization is achieved and for Mill's skepticism as to the value and stability of present civilization.

In general, Mill uses the term "civilization" loosely. Basically, he has in mind economic development, as standing at the heart of modern civilization. Such development, however, has a number of troubling aspects. As he reminds us in his *Principles of Economics*, "The increase of wealth is not boundless."[3] This is not all bad in Mill's view, because "the trampling, crushing, elbowing, and treading on each other's heels, which form the existing type of social life" is hardly the most desirable lot of mankind. Mill, who daringly flirted with socialist ideas, prefers a stationary state, admittedly at a high level of material wealth, in which he and all others can turn to cultivation, that is, the pursuit of culture.

In short, much inspired by Coleridge, who, as Mill tells us, inquired "[h]ow far mankind have gained by civilization," he goes beyond his utilitarian beginnings and questions the basic assumptions of economic development.[4] In the process, he also questions the "virtue" of the middle class, the only class to benefit so far from "progress," for the lower classes have not seen their lot improved. Mill's essay is a far cry from Guizot's encomium of civilization and its "moral" middle-class bearers. Thus, we have both a piece of analysis—the motor of the present-day civilizing process is economic development—and a judgment—its results are tainted with the immoral.

As I remarked earlier, Mill is not always consistent. For example, in his classic and admirable essay *On Liberty* (1859), he defends the right of the Mormons to their own beliefs, such as their belief in polygamy, and asserts that "I am not aware that any community has a right to force another to be civilized."[5] Even if civilization were all good, and we have seen that Mill doubted this, others cannot be forced to undergo the civilizing process. Neither the colonial nor European (racist) version of the mission can be imposed upon them.[6]

Yet in his *Considerations on Representative Government*, published two years after *On Liberty*, Mill defends colonial rule (he worked for a good part of his life in the East India Company's London office), describing it "as legitimate as any other if it is the one which in the existing state of civilisation of the subject people most facilitates their transition to a higher stage of improvement.

There are . . . conditions of society in which a vigorous despotism
is in itself the best mode of government for training the people in
what is specifically wanting to render them capable of a higher
civilisation."[7]

My intent is not to judge Mill's position as such—perhaps
despotic Ataturks may sometimes be essential for dragging their
people toward "civilization"—nor to make fun of his to-ing and
fro-ing—who, other than a monomaniac, is free of that tendency?—but to underline how, unlike some of the figures discussed in the preceding chapter, Mill is aware of the defects in the
results of the civilizing process, although generally in favor of it
(and thus different from those like Rousseau, for example, who
condemn it root and branch). This is one reason why I have included him in this chapter. As a representative liberal thinker, he
is aware of the two faces of civilization and not merely a devotee
of the European ideology.

The other reason emerges from some of his comments in his
essay on Coleridge. It is Coleridge, Mill tells us, who reminds us
how precarious civilization is and "what a host of civilizing and
restraining influences," are necessary for the existence of "a state
of things so repugnant to man's self-will and love of independence." With all its flaws, it is implied, civilization is a good thing,
whose preservation "demands the continuance of those influences
as the condition of its own existence."[8] Mill, whether Freud had
read this part of him or not, was raising the same concern about
the thin veneer that overlaid the civilizing process. As a process
based primarily on economic development in recent times, carrying with it doubts as to its moral rightness, the product, civilization, was by no means certain to persist or to develop further. It
is, rather, a subject of anxiety and doubt.

3

Freud's *Civilization and Its Discontents*, originally published in 1930, is about an abstraction, rather than about particular civilizations. In fact, of course, it reflects the European situation in which Freud lived. Although Mill's essay on civilization may not have had a direct influence on Freud, it was part of the intellectual context in which the latter moved. In this setting, Gobineau's racial theories carried an implicit threat to Freud, a Jew (in spite of Gobineau's praise of the Jews). More contemporary and intellectually pertinent was the work of Darwin, for Freud was in essence a Darwinian carrying out the inquiry into cultural evolution that the earlier biologist had started. Then there was Freud's doppelgänger, Nietzsche, whose nihilistic comments on civilization would have been known to Freud, although he claimed not to have read him. Along with Nietzsche, there is the shadow of Le Bon, with his anxiety about the dark, threatening masses, the internal barbarians of the times. And, not to be overlooked, Conrad's Kurtz and the "heart of darkness."

It is Freud's overall view that civilization is a repressive burden that brings unhappiness and lies heavily on the human spirit. This is the prevalent note in his accounts. In its briefest form, his argument is that civilization is necessarily based on coercion and the renunciation of instinct; indeed, we can regard "instinctual repression as a measure of the level of civilization that has been reached."[9] One result is that modern civilization represents the tightening of the screws of unconscious guilt. "If civilization is a necessary course of development from the family to humanity as a whole, then—as a result of the inborn conflict arising from ambivalence, of the eternal struggle between the trends of love and death—there is inextricably bound up with it an increase of the sense of guilt, which will perhaps reach heights that the individual finds hard to tolerate," Freud declares, connecting his argument to a Kantian notion of widening social bonds.[10]

Since Freud was working out his theories at a time when the dominant mental disease was identified as the vague entity "neurasthenia," his "analysis" was very much in the spirit of his age. His argument is as follows. Civilization arises in the face of a threatening reality, both outside and inside. To survive, humans must learn to conquer their physical environment. This they do by means of technology and eventually science. At one point, Freud calls man the "prosthetic God." To quell internal anxiety, humans turn to alcohol, drugs, yoga, asceticism, religion, science—and civilization. It is all in vain. Humanity by its very nature is condemned to discontent and unhappiness.[11] Stoicism is the recommended stance in the face of this bleak analysis.

4

In seeking to understand Freud's analysis of civilization, it is essential to remember that he starts from a clinical basis. It is his work as a psychoanalyst with patients that underlies what he has to say about larger social topics, such as civilization. Thus it is through the interpretation of his patients' dreams about childhood that Freud comes to the great realization that "behind this childhood of the individual we are promised a picture of the phylogenetic childhood—a picture of the development of the human race, of which the individual's development is in fact an abbreviated recapitulation influenced by the chance circumstances of life."[12]

Civilization, therefore, is simply the individual and his development writ large. Leaving aside the methodological problems entwined with this leap, we note that only by an immersion in

Freud's total theory can we make sense of his assertion. That large task is not one I wish to undertake here. Instead, I shall simply mention the prominent role of sex (especially infantile sex), repression, the unconscious, various defense mechanisms, such as displacement, denial, projection, and complexes, such as the Oedipus complex, and assume that the interested reader will pursue these topics elsewhere.

Instead of going into these details, I shall turn back to *Civilization and Its Discontents* itself. First of all, the book must be seen as a continuation of *The Future of an Illusion*, written a few years earlier. That book was concerned with religion. Freud's treatment of religion is dismissive. As he comments in his later book *Moses and Monotheism* (1939), psychoanalysis "leads us to a result that reduces religion to the status of a neurosis of mankind and explains its grandiose powers in the same way as we should a neurotic obsession in our individual patients."[13] This "reduction" was first carried out in *The Future of an Illusion*, as indicated in its title.

Freud's dismissal of religion as neurosis and illusion evoked a letter from his friend the novelist Romain Rolland, who chided Freud for thinking of religion only in terms of Christianity, with its God the Father, and thus its Oedipal possibilities. Instead, Rolland proposed what he called the "oceanic feeling" as being at the core of religion. Freud replied to his "aquatic" friend, as he called Rolland, with a book from his "terrestrial" friend: the book was *Civilization and Its Discontents*.

Here, Freud broadened the argument. The subject was now civilization, of which religion was merely one part, one attempted palliative to the general unhappiness resulting from our living in society. I would argue, however, that religion is still at the center of Freud's concern and not merely a part of it. Whether one

agrees with this interpretation or not, it is well to recall the role of religion in the original conception of "civilization" by Mirabeau. The French eighteenth-century thinker, along with most who followed after him, such as Burke and Guizot, emphasized both its centrality and its necessity in the establishment and maintenance of civilization. Calling religion into question, Freud was logically led to a pessimistic view of civilization.

Looking back at his work when he was seventy-nine, Freud wrote in his *Autobiography* that in *Totem and Taboo*, he had sought "to make use of the newly discovered findings of analysis in order to investigate the origins of religion and morality." With his later works, "I perceived ever more clearly that the events of human history, the interactions between human nature, cultural development and the precipitates of primaeval experiences (*the most prominent example of which is religion* [emphasis added]) are no more than a reflection of the dynamic conflicts between the ego, the id, and the super-ego . . . are the very same processes repeated upon a wider stage."[14]

Freud's motives were consistent. In his lifelong quest to supplant religion with science, and thus have humanity grow out of its childhood, he eroded the services of religion in civilization. As he asks, if religion "had succeeded in making happy the greater part of humanity, in consoling them, in reconciling them to life, and into making them supporters of civilization, then no one would dream of striving to alter existing conditions. But instead of this what do we see? We see that an appallingly large number of men are discontented with civilization and unhappy with it." The solution is "to replace the consequences of repression by the results of rational mental effort, as in the analytic treatment of neurotics."[15] In short, Freud wishes for a civilization based on science and its way of thinking. True, Freud had already numbered

science among the would-be palliatives for unhappiness, and, like the others, unable to bring us happiness. Yet at least it forces us to face reality, and then to learn to live with it.

Like Gobineau before him, Freud thought he had solved the riddle of history. One last quotation here can serve to support this assertion. "[T]he meaning of the evolution of civilization is no longer obscure to us," Freud proclaims. "It must present the struggle between Eros and Death, between the instinct of life and the instinct of destruction, as it works itself out in the human species. This struggle is what all life essentially consists of, and the evolution of civilization may therefore be simply described as the struggle for life of the human species for existence."[16] Having labeled Gobineau as monomaniacal, it is hard not to place Freud in the same category. Race for one, religion for the other: they appear obsessed.

Of course, there are powerful differences. Freud's work is grounded in clinical observations that are of scientific value. His theories, based on the observations, are part of a new science of the mind, with various of the theories, although highly controversial, strong contenders for acceptance when suitably modified. His "speculations" arising from his observations and theories are always exciting and stimulate further thought. His continuation of Darwin—studying further the struggle of the human species for existence—however precarious, is, in my view, heading in the right direction.

The problem, of course, is that Freud overspeculates, making, for example, a grand leap from individual psychological processes to group ones without being aware of the fundamental differences between the two sets of phenomena. In this part of his work, Freud is a "great simplifier," to use Jacob Burckhardt's term. Similarly, he falls victim as did so many in his time and af-

ter to the misleading notion of recapitulation. So, too, he tends to fall into the trap of reductionism.

The charges made above, and similar ones, can be brought against Freud in regard to what he has to say about civilization. His "analysis," as said earlier, is mainly of an abstraction. The Freud who fervently collected archeological specimens was not really interested in historical civilizations. Well, so be it. Although it goes against the whole thrust of my book, which is seeking to understand civilization as a concrete historical development, in principle there is no reason not to try to understand civilization "philosophically," as a matter of general laws. The problem is that even if this is a justifiable approach, Freud is not really interested in civilization itself. It is a Trojan Horse concept, a cover under which he continues to mount his critique of religion.

With so much to criticize, why is Freud so important for our topic? One simple reason is that he has grabbed people's imagination in a profound way. He has obviously touched upon something deep in our unconscious, our resentment of the constrictions of "civilized" existence. We are all Huckleberry Finns at some level, wanting to "light out for the territory" and freedom. Then there is the "spirit of the age." Freud was writing after World War I had revealed some of modern civilization's hideous consequences. Within a few years, Hitler was to come to power in Germany. The sense that civilization was cracking, that it was a thin veneer over the bestial lurking beneath each individual and all of society, was widespread. Freud seems to explain why.

More than anyone else, it seems, Freud gave voice to the realization that civilization necessarily had a dark side to it. And he seemed to bring at the very least a patina of science to this dire conclusion. Asserting his analysis about all civilization—the abstraction—his admonitions clearly applied also to the specific one of his own surroundings. Most immediately, the European claim to superiority was cut off in the most far-reaching manner.

Yet from the ruins of Freud's work on civilization emerged a contribution to its further development. Perhaps, as a paradoxical consequence of his work, we need to look at civilization not so much as an abstract, timeless concept, but as a process, constantly at work? What is and has been the "civilizing process" that led eighteenth-century European man to reify its result and make it into a possession, even while it was constantly changing in his hands? Freud's fecund contribution to this problem was to assert that the individual grew up to rational adulthood by a process of repression, sublimation, and other such psychological mechanisms, whereby instinct was replaced by reason, violent expression of feelings by cautious conciliation of interests. Following this line of thought, we need only apply a similar mode of analysis to the civilizing process as it works with groups and in actual historical circumstances. This, in fact, is the route taken by our next figure, Norbert Elias, the author of a book called *The Civilizing Process*.

5

Elias has already been mentioned in Chapter 1. We need now to give more attention to his work and the light it sheds on our topic of civilization. The two volumes of his masterpiece *The Civilizing Process* are titled *The History of Manners* and *Power and Civility*, the second being a study of the rise of the absolutist state.[17] As we shall see, the two subjects are intrinsically connected.

In volume 1, Elias has a long and interesting section at the beginning on the differences between *Kultur* and *Zivilization*, especially in Germany. This is worth reading for itself, but is not essential for our purposes. (The notions of culture, *Bildung*, folk, and locality versus civilization, mechanization, cosmopolitanism, and universalism, as epitomized in the clash of German and French thinking, have already been touched on.) What concerns us here is Elias's thesis that civilization as an achieved state is less important than the process that results in that state (which, in this perspective, is necessarily in a state of change).

Elias was heavily influenced by Freud, but, as a sociologist, or rather a philosophical or historical sociologist, he thought that Freud's concept of human psychology was ahistorical. What I have said above about *Civilization and Its Discontents*, with its focus on an abstraction, concurs with this view. In contrast, Elias saw civilization as a historical development, subject to empirical inquiry, which then needed to be placed in the service of theory. In fact, of course, theory was already involved in the way one went about doing the empirical research.

The overall theory Elias brought to his work on the civilizing process has generally been called figurational sociology (although Elias came to prefer the term "process sociology"). In his words: "This simple and precise formulation expresses well how from the interweaving of countless individual interests and intentions— whether tending in the same direction or in divergent and hostile directions—something comes into being that was planned and intended by none of these individuals, yet has emerged nevertheless from their intentions and actions. And really this is the whole secret of social figurations."[18] In itself, this formulation is not new; it is what lies behind Adam Smith's invisible hand. What is new is Elias's application of the idea to the study of civilization.

Essentially combining Freud and Adam Smith (although without invoking the latter's name), Elias argues in original terms that during the civilizing process, the individual and the society change together. Each forms part of the other. A civilized person is necessary for a civilization. What is external—the rules of society imposed on the individual as he or she grows up—becomes internalized in typical Freudian fashion. For example, the child is taught to feel shame over his or her unrestrained bowel movements and unconsciously extends this feeling to related products. Elias, who himself had undergone psychoanalytic therapy and had led group therapy sessions, had learned his lesson well.

The task now was to apply it historically. In the European court societies of the fourteenth and fifteenth centuries, the aristocracy was taught to avoid belching, farting, and other such bodily expressions, and to be "mannered." Such behavior set them off from their crude inferiors, who were perceived as still in an animalic rather than civilized state. On an even more important level in regard to civilization, the restraint of impulses to violence was instituted, and reason and contrivance were substituted for instinct and its outbreaks. As we know, thinking back, for example, to Mirabeau, the restraint of violence is one of the key building blocks of civilization. Whereas others saw religion as the force involved, Elias sees manners. He was also aware that restraint of instinct in whatever form also brought about the loss of certain kinds of personal freedom.

The other force essential to the development being described was the state. The growth of central power was a historical necessity, a condition of the restraint of aristocratic aggression. As indicated, Elias's second volume was on the absolutist state. It was this state that also fostered the growth of the bourgeoisie, as a counterweight to the aristocracy. An unintended result, of course, was the coming to power of the middle classes in the centuries that followed, with the civilizing process, and hence the form of civilization, extended to larger segments of the society.

In sum, the civilizing process entailed a historical development in which personality, social change, and the state are all correlated—in unintended fashion. Elias spells out these developments in a detailed manner, from which I have taken only a few pieces. His books must be read for themselves. They are fundamental contributions to the study of a process that continues today. Although Elias does not engage in the task, his work can also be applied to other than European societies to describe and analyze the process of their coming to civilization.

Criticisms, of course, can be made of Elias's work. As he presents it, the process seems unique to Europe; but I have already indicated that it can and has been extended elsewhere. As noted earlier, one can see evidences of the civilizing process in Europe itself before the centuries studied by Elias. He can be accused of neglecting the role of trade as a civilizing force. In a typical comment, the eighteenth-century English writer Joseph Addison declared that "we are not a little obliged to Trade, as it has been a great means of civilizing our Nation, and banishing out of it all the Remains of its antient Barbarity."[19] This was almost a cliché of Enlightened thought, and Voltaire and numerous others could be cited along the same lines. Yet Elias seems to neglect this line of inquiry. In another direction, Elias turned a blind eye to the decivilizing process, the way in which civilization could break down; and this with the example of the Nazis all around him.

Legitimate as such criticisms may be, they should not distract us from Elias's achievement. Taken with the utmost seriousness as a scholar, as he should be, he changes the discourse on civilization. Following upon Freud, he, too, implicitly undermines the claim to superiority of the European version (although his own historical example is that of Europe). Elias was well aware of the importance of his subject. The word "civilization," he said, "sums

up everything in which Western society of the last two or three
centuries believes itself superior to earlier societies or 'more
primitive' contemporary ones." Going beyond Freud, however,
Elias has turned the question about civilization into an issue for
social science and historical investigation.[20] It is this spirit of inquiry that hovers, or should hover, over all future work on the
question of civilization.

6

Mill, Freud, and Elias have allowed us to look at the European
discourse about civilization from an angle different from that offered by the figures discussed in the previous chapter. Rather
than an epiphany. we seem to hear the strains of what is closer to
being a threnody. At the very least, the triumphant tone is gone.

With Mill we have a thinker close to the center of the establishment in England, epitomizing its liberal aspirations and beliefs. Yet, seeking to combine the views of Bentham and Coleridge, he offers us an ambivalent position on civilization. He
clearly values it, and he situates it along with the idea of progress
as an achievement of European man (and woman). He even
thinks it is something that can be imposed on colonial peoples for
their own good. Equating the process to a large extent with economic development, however, he casts doubt upon the latter's
moral value, and inclines toward a semi-socialist, stationary society. By questioning the basic value of his contemporary capitalist
surroundings, he also shakes the foundations of both European
civilization and the process that brings it into being.

Freud goes even further. On the basis of his new science of
psychoanalysis, he argues that civilization is necessarily repressive,
and thus a carrier of unhappiness. It is, so to speak, blighted at its
core. A consequence of humanity's efforts to survive and master

its environment—Freud is very Darwinian—it enacts a heavy psychic price in the form of guilt. Indeed, that price is at its highest, perhaps at an intolerable level, in contemporary European civilization. Freud, however, is also a scientific rationalist—attacking religion as much as civilization in his books—who places ego above the instincts, thus establishing his own ambivalence about civilization as an abstraction. In this mode of thinking, he worries about civilization as a flimsy covering placed over the raging passions, which may crack at any moment. In this complicated manner, Freud's analysis of essential discontent is both about his own European civilization and about *any* civilization and its discontents. As such, his theory necessarily constitutes a part of any future account of civilization and its content.

Psychoanalysis strongly influenced Elias, who placed it in the service of his work as a sociologist. Taking Freud's account of human psychic development, Elias uses it as a model for the way society itself develops, at the same time shaping the individuals who comprise it. Repression of instinct is central to both accounts. Repairing Freud's lack of historical perspective, Elias applies the schema to what he calls the civilizing process in Europe of the fourteenth and fifteenth centuries. Linking court society, the aristocracy, and the early growth of the absolutist state, he seeks to show in empirical detail how a refined, mannered society developed. The result was what Mirabeau and his contemporaries in the eighteenth century came to call civilization. What Elias adds to their concept is an emphasis on process, rather than a static end result, and he thus weakens, if not destroys, the ideological support for European superiority based on race or any other essentialist notion.

Taken together, these three thinkers—Mill, Freud, and Elias—are representative of a turn in the discourse of civilization within Europe itself. In the beginning, that is, their own times, their voices were those of a minority. Even among intellectuals, let alone the "masses," civilization tended to be viewed as an unquestioned good, and as a European achievement. Only with time did the voices of discontent swell, amplified by the thunderous evil of World War I and subsequent other evidence of the decivilizing possibilities inherent in civilization's European version. Such challenges, however, must not obscure the fact that it is civilization itself and its various forms that continue to constitute the battlefield on which divergent opinions clash.

5

Other Civilizations

1

So far, our main focus has been on European civilization, as if that were the only contender to the civilized state. As I remarked at the very beginning of this book, however, there are other claimants to the awareness that their society was different from that of the barbarians outside. Thus, the Chinese saw themselves as inhabiting a "Middle Kingdom," the Romans spoke of the Pax Romana, and the Arabs, with Ibn Khaldun leading the way, thought in terms of the city and the nomad. From our present vantage point, we can now recognize these formulations as in some way synonyms for the term "civilization." This recognition should not obscure the difference: "civilization" as a reified term emerges in the eighteenth century, in the West, and only then is applied retroactively to other "civilizations."

Two points are important here. The first is that there were civilizations, great and small, before the European in the eighteenth century. To varying degrees, these civilizations were aware of their status, indeed, self-aware as to their "superiority" to other or noncivilized groups. The second point, however, is that the degree of self-awareness, and the context in which it developed, which led to the reification of civilization with all its claims, such as we have been grappling with in the preceding chapters, emerged only a few centuries ago, in a European form. This statement does not denigrate what we now view as other civilizations. It simply places the concept of civilization in a historical frame and allows for its consideration on a global basis.

As I have indicated in Chapter 4, the claim to the obvious superiority of European civilization was shaken both internally, by thinkers such as Mill, Freud, and Elias (different examples could be adduced, and even before them there were challenges by Montaigne, Rousseau, and others, when Europe was still at the beginning of its rise to power), and externally, by its world wars, basically civil (although uncivilized) in nature. Nevertheless, for all practical purposes, until the end of World War II the notion of the superiority of European civilization largely prevailed. Even as a ghost, it exercised a kind of ghastly power.

To pursue the vicissitudes of the civilization concept in regard to other than the European version, I shall look first at what is perhaps a rather unexpected example, the recovery/discovery of ancient civilizations, especially Egyptian civilization, as part of the constituting of European civilization's sense of itself. This began as an early nineteenth-century experience. Next, I shall try to illustrate how the concept of civilization radiated out beyond Europe, starting apparently after the mid nineteenth century. I shall take Japan as my prime example, followed by a quick glance at China and Thailand. Again, my method is one of comparison, shedding light on the phenomenon from different points.

2

In 1798, Napoleon landed in Egypt. Whereas Captain Cook, for example, had had a few scientists aboard his vessels in his explorations in the South Seas a quarter century earlier, the French general's ships carried an entourage of something like 152 scientists, scholars, and other officials to help him "explore" the country. Although his purpose was conquest, as part of the battle against the British, another intention was the acquisition of scientific knowledge. This quest was and is, as I have already tried to show, a defining aspect of European civilization.

In the event, Napoleon did not hold on to Egypt. However, with the discovery of the Rosetta Stone in 1799 and its subsequent translation, a key was unexpectedly found into a whole other world: that of ancient Egyptian civilization. Thus was conquered a long-ago "land" and "life" of past times that became part of European civilization's "holdings," stored in museums, archived in books, and even given visual representation in Paris in the form of an obelisk in the place de la Concorde. A continuity of material use, life habits, religious attitudes and artistic style, occurring in the flood plains of the Nile, and, stretching over almost 4,000 years, seemed to warrant the designation "culture" or "civilization," with the two often used as synonyms.

A few decades after the discovery of ancient Egypt, similar finds were made in other parts of what has come to be called the Middle East. Mesopotamia (as named by the Greeks, but variously called Sumer, Akkad, Babylonia, and Assyria by its inhabitants) became an equal claimant to the title of first civilization. Around 1820–21, the first scientific examination of Nineveh, a great Assyrian city, was begun, and in 1840 the British archaeologist Sir Austen Henry Layard started the excavations that moved the field of archaeology to an entirely new level. In the process, the wonderful carved figures of ancient Egypt were matched by the powerful wall sculptures of the Assyrian king dom. Both

Egypt and Mesopotamia became contenders for the title of having been the first to have an alphabet and other manifestations of civilization.

That fight, and its like, is not one in which I want to engage. While the general view is that what we have come to call civilization arose first in the areas that are now Syria, Iraq, and Egypt, all else is in contention (and there are some who would wish to look upon China as the birthplace of civilization). Instead, we need only to bear in mind for our purposes such questions as: Did civilizations arise spontaneously and independently, or was there one source from which they diffused? Whatever their differences in detail, did these early societies all have common features, and lastly, did they all have common causes?

Rather than trying to answer these questions in strict sequence or with any certainty, I shall simply posit certain assumptions. The primary condition for the emergence of "civilization" was a major climate change about 12,000 years ago, which made possible a profound shift in the condition of the human species, so that hunter-gatherers gradually became agriculturists. From that transformation followed many of the features that we recognize as forming a civilization: fixed settlements, shortly becoming cities, walled about; surplus production, allowing for different social strata—warriors, priests, artisans, and traders, along with farmers; an agricultural surplus that permitted differentiated power, as well as complicated crafts and art; the development of early "sciences" such as astronomy; an increasing population; and the development of large armies and more effective weapons.

The specifics of archaeological excavations are constantly challenging our received ideas of when something first appeared and where and how it spread—in general pushing everything further into the past. Fascinating as these finds are, we must not let them distract us from our concern with the concept of civilization. These ancient civilizations are only known to us *as such* as a result of the workings of European civilization (which is itself, of course, the result of innumerable exchanges with and influences of other and often earlier "civilizations," as we would call them today). These civilizations are not "native" to the peoples now inhabiting the areas in which the past is being dug up (although increasingly these peoples are now repossessing their own past) but have been conjured up by prehistorical and historical studies that constitute part of what present-day civilization is about.

In its self-reflexivity, resulting in the eighteenth-century invention of the concept of civilization, Europe prepared the way for its relations with other civilizations. This could be, for example, in the form of coexistence, attempted conquest, simply keeping them at arm's length, or combinations of the three. What was unavoidable was the *recognition* of these "other civilizations." In the case of ancient civilizations, they were literally excavated from the past, and thus given new life. In this revived form, they were ingested into European civilization itself, cannibalized, so to speak. Only then were they returned to humanity at large.

3

Rather than continue in this vein, I want to focus on Egyptian civilization as my exemplar of ancient civilizations. Its particular variant of the overall cause leading to civilization was "an increasingly arid climate" that "first began to make it more profitable for men to forsake the nomadic life of the open plains and confine their activities to the vicinity of the river."[1] Here in the rich lands made possible by the periodic flooding of the Nile, early Neolithic peoples turned to agriculture, the raising of domesticated animals, the building of houses and towns, the use of pottery vessels for the storage of food, the weaving of cloth, and the shaping of tools, in short much of the paraphernalia we identify with civilization. Artificial irrigation and land reclamation provided great surpluses beyond subsistence needs.

After a prehistory that we can now date back to about 8,000 B.C., Egypt enters history proper around 3,200 B.C., in the so-called Early Dynastic Period. It continues through recorded dynastic periods until the last native dynasty, ending in 341 B.C., or, better, 332 B.C. and the conquest of the country by Alexander the Great. Thus, for almost 3,500 years, through periods labeled the Old, Middle, and New Kingdoms by present-day scholars, and innumerable dynasties within them, something recognizable as Egyptian civilization flourished and declined, but persisted.[2] According to my knowledgeable friends, the terms *misr*, *mesr*, and *masreya* were the Egyptian synonyms for our word "civilization."

As a kingdom, Egypt waxed and waned over the centuries and millennia. Sometimes its center was in Lower Egypt, near the Delta, sometimes in Upper Egypt, that is, south of the cataracts and toward Nubia (lower and upper being equated with north and south in our mapping terms makes for confusion). A major expansion and consolidation occurred when the two areas were united into one kingdom. At different times, different cities were the major locus of power: Heliopolis, Memphis, Herakleopolis, Thebes. At various points in time, Egypt made excursions into Nubia to the south or Syria and lands to the north. At most times, it was engaged in vigorous trade with its neighbors and lands beyond.

What characterized this civilization, constant and recognizable over time, although with constant changes as well? We only know about it through its remains and ruins. These, fortunately, are abundant, for Egypt was gifted with stone (in contrast to its Mesopotamian neighbors), which the Egyptians used for enormous monuments that have lasted to our time. On these monuments were hieroglyphics and figures, and with the finding of the Rosetta Stone, an understanding of their meaning became possible.

There is no mistaking the flat-faced, flat-footed figures in the hieroglyphic stone, or the hieroglyphs themselves, as being anything but survivals from Egyptian civilization. It is a style, a form of representation, that stamps them so for eternity. And "eternity" is the key word. It appears that the ancient Egyptians were as much concerned with death as with life. In fact, for them there seems to have been an unbroken continuity. Every king (and queens when they reigned) built a sumptuous tomb, generally in the form of a pyramid, for himself and his family members, replete with the goods of this world to sustain him in the next. On the walls of his tomb were pictures of those who would continue to serve him in the nether world, handing him food or raiment. Actual foods were also provided, along with utensils, often laid out on a table. Rods of office, weapons, all the other accoutrements of his actual reign were placed beside him.

It was not just the royal person, however, who built for eternity in this fashion. Around him would be the high courtiers and officials who had served him in life, with their own tombs and furnishings. Even humbler people had their provisions for the afterlife. All peoples have to confront the consciousness of death. The Egyptian way was an abiding and omnipresent incorporation of that other state into the present one of life. The unintended result was that in the pyramids and tombs, in the mummies and their supplies, and in the metabae and stelae, and all the

other installations to aid in the crossing over, Egyptian civilization has come alive in our own present, at least since the end of
the eighteenth century.

In general, it has come to us in fragments. Yet, just as Cuvier
in the early nineteenth century was putting together evolutionary
species from bits and pieces, so early archaeologists and their successors have been able to reconstruct an entire civilization in extraordinary detail. Putting the details together reveals a civilizational whole. We even know, for example, which kings looted the
tombs of their predecessors to build parts of their own tombs. We
know the names of the kings' harem girls. More important, we
know the names of the gods—Horus, Isis, and so forth—and
their functions in firming up the king's rule in this life and pro-
tecting him in the next, or, as the Egyptians would have put it,
continuing life.

Stepping back from the fragments, the whole that we see allows us to discern the full figure of Egyptian civilization. In its
prime state, lasting for many centuries, the first thing that we
should be aware of is its enormous wealth. What other civilization could have poured so much of its material, manpower, and
time—its social capital—into the construction of structures that
have no other function than to consecrate death? Yet sufficient
capital remained to finance an affluent life for the rich and a relatively secure life for the poor. And even to mount expeditions to
conquer other peoples and lands.

What of the role of religion? The ancient Egyptians had a
multitude of divinities. There are indications that many of the
gods of prehistoric times were "vicious and uncivilized beings
whose savagery was appeased by human sacrifice and other
bloody rites."[3] What we see appears to be a process in which religion is itself "civilized," while simultaneously acting as a civi-

lizing influence. The gods themselves become guardians of a lawful and moral order. Where once women and servants of a chieftain had been slain and then buried with him, now figurines representing them were placed in the tomb. Egyptian civilization did not reach to a national or monotheistic religion (with the brief exception of Akhnaton), and thus to what we would recognize as a great religion. It did, however, provide guardians to accompany one into the life-in-death that characterizes so much of this civilization's life.

Other features are the development of writing and the alphabet. The latter appears to date from around 1900 to 1800 B.C., and there is much controversy over whether the innovation first occurred in Egypt or in Mesopotamia. Using papyrus or writing on stone, ancient Egyptians achieved immortality in this unexpected form. A defining feature of civilization as contrasted to barbarism, as we have noted from the beginning, is language. And writing is an even more fundamental distinction than the babbling of words by the uncivilized.

To avoid a paragraph on each feature, I shall simply more or less list defining attributes of civilization as found among the Egyptians. We have already touched on pyramids and tombs, the former being extraordinary feats of building, in some cases unrivaled since then—the great pyramid is still the largest building ever constructed. To these should be added obelisks and temples. Calendars and the use of astronomy are to be noted. Overall, there is government and its various agencies, supervising land reclamation, the provision of food, the shipments of grain, and trade in general. Fighting and warfare were a central element, manifested in the establishing of forts and the improvement of weapons. On a more mundane level, we find clothing of various sorts, mostly linen, and the washing of both the clothes and their wearers. More glittering, but on the same level, we find exquisite jewelry and all sorts of other adornments for both sexes.

Lastly, perhaps, we must consider the realm of art. Its stylistic level varied over time, and is, of course, also a matter of judgment. Still, it seems clear that there were peaks and valleys, with some artisans better trained and more talented than others. But their objects were not created to be art objects. The stone sculptures, for example, were made to be representations of the dead, or as duplicates of what would accompany them into their living deaths. It is for us that they are beautiful works of art. How much of an aesthetic response they aroused in their ancient viewers is difficult or impossible to tell. Yet this art, however perceived, seems an intrinsic part of the civilization that was once Egypt's.

Without saying anything further about that civilization per se, I want to reiterate how it was both discovered and conquered by the European civilization of modern times. It is an "other" civilization, a past one made alive by recent excavations and re- constructions, helping to define what we mean by civilization. Its features, although particular in nature, are those to be en- countered in any civilization. Only in retrospect, however, do we recognize it as a "civilization." Once so recognized, it be- comes part of European civilization itself. Its death has become part of our life.

4

It was not only the past that suddenly produced civilizations. In the latter part of the nineteenth century, the European concept spread outward, conjuring up other "civilizations" by accultura- tion. Either as a new conception of their past or as an aspiration to a future, numerous non-Western societies suddenly had to cope with the question of civilization. The first and, in many ways, prototypical case is that of Japan. I want to deal with it in further detail, with some reference to other cases, such as China and Thailand.

It was shortly after Perry's ships opened up Japan to Western commerce and ideas that a Japanese word for civilization, *bun-mei-kaika*, appeared. It has persisted, and in the form of *hikaku bunmeiron* (the comparative theory of civilization) occupies Japanese scholars to this day. Typical was a major panel at the 1991 conference in Japan of the Social and Economic History Society that devoted itself entirely to trying to define Japan as a civilization. Haunting the discussion, one ethnologist tells us, was "a desire to escape from the Eurocentric worldview which has dominated the study of history since the eighteenth century." The reason this effort is so important is, as our ethnologist informs us, that "if there is one concept that has a privileged place in the ethnocentric images through which Western peoples see themselves in relation to others, it is the concept of civilization."[4] Civilization, in short, as we have already intuited, is hardly a neutral term, but comes bearing value-laden meanings.

It also comes bearing a challenge. How do other cultures and societies, with their own claims to being "civilized" respond? In what manner do they adapt, adopt, or reject? The example of Japan is especially illuminating. Different elements in Japanese society, of course, responded differently to Perry's ships in 1853. Some wished to close the doors, both materially and spiritually. Others recognized that material rejection was impossible if Japan wished to survive as an independent nation. Consequently, as one Japanese conservative put it, Japan should espouse a combination of "Eastern morality and Western technology." Claiming that while the West might be superior in science and technology, he insisted that the East excelled in its ethical teachings.[5] Still others saw that a spiritual, or cultural, revolution was as necessary as a scientific one. Thus, in the Meiji period, some of the key figures in the government went to Europe to learn and returned home imbued with the idea that the only way Japan could keep its independence *and* take its rightful place in history was fully to embrace Western civilization. Theirs was a reverse "missionary" expedition.

They undertook their task in the name of *keimo*, or Enlightenment. In their own terms, I would argue, they sought to repeat the early experience of European modernity, waging the same battle for a rejection of the binding authority of tradition and taking as their definition of civilization the Kantian notion of critique: as one scholar, Fukuzawa Yukichi, defines that notion, "Doubts generated from within oneself." In more positive terms, they believed that they could change the structure of society itself by reason.[6] Repudiating their past as "barbaric," they also sought to locate their own place in a larger pattern of history: the history of civilization. In doing so, they emphasized educational reforms, the abolition of feudal society and its myriad ranks, and the need to involve all strata of society in the leap to "civilization." To a large extent, the result of their efforts was that a small island, with a limited population, was launched on a path that would bring it in the twentieth century to a position of being the world's second or third most powerful entity, certainly in economic terms.

In fact, the Japanese enlightened reformers did not succeed in doing away with tradition. Accompanying their reading of Guizot, whose works, along with those of the English historian Henry Thomas Buckle, had been quickly translated, the reformers still retained the teachings of the sages, adapting the foreign and native texts to one another, and making them compatible. In addition, they had to fight against the danger of inferiority feel-

ings (just as did the American colonists faced with British civilization a century earlier) and to take pride in their own deeds and
culture. It is noteworthy that one Japanese scholar says of Guizot:
"What he calls the 'natural' meaning of 'world' civilization is thus
nothing 'natural' but is constructed in his discursive act of ex-
cluding Asia from the category of civilization."[7] In the end, the
particular way in which the Japanese achieved what I would like
to call their "accivilization" appears unique, although characterized by ubiquitous features. (Let us note, in passing, that cultures
are subject to acculturation. Is it a mark of our thinking about
civilizations that there is no comparable word, such as "accivilization," the one I have tried to introduce, to express what is, in fact,
their historically permeable nature?) It is only in the light, however, of a "comparative theory of civilization," to use the words of
a present-day Japanese scholar, that we can tell exactly how
unique that process has been.

5

To these brief remarks on how the concept of civilization was
transmitted to Japan and how it was received and developed, I
want to add only a few general observations. The first is to note
how strongly the subject of civilization is connected to the theme
of modernity. In some cases, the two are almost treated as synonyms. Perhaps a subtle difference is that civilization is a state to
be achieved, and modernity is a process by which to achieve it.

One part of modernity is perceived as nation-building, and the
retention of Japan's independence. Thus, one scholar, Fukuzawa
Yukichi, declared during the debates on the new learning: "Our
task now is to promote civilisation with a definite objective in
view—and that is to distinguish clearly between our own country
and others in such a way that we may preserve the independence

of our own country. The only means of thus preserving our independence is to adopt western civilisation." Fukuzawa was no narrow nationalist. He realized that, like all other nations, Japan's task was also to contribute to civilization at large. However, he wryly went on to say that "in the present state of the world we are prevented by the conditions of international relations from considering these noble ends."[8]

The only way that Japan could take its rightful place in the international system was by becoming "civilized." This, in turn, meant adopting the standards of civilization that defined the international system; and these, of course, meant the European definition. If Japan wanted, for example, to have the freedom to set its own tariffs as part of its modernizing effort, it had to "join" the reigning international system.[9] To oppose unequal treaties, executed in the face of Western military superiority, meant achieving equality as a "civilized state" in regard to international law, and the embrace of such notions as the inviolability of sovereignty.

Civilization meant changes in institutions, such as the penal system and its prisons. Thus, the early Meiji leaders sent three prison officials to visit the British penal systems in India, Hong Kong, and Singapore. It meant establishing a diplomatic corps and very quickly learning that Western custom dictated Western-style dress rather than the traditional kimonos. It meant the embrace of a wide range of military initiatives, borrowing from the West. And it meant an openness to Western thought and culture of an almost unprecedented nature.

The Japanese were sensitive to the ideology of racism accompanying European civilization and went to great efforts to counter the notion of racial inferiority. Thus, to cite a trivial example, they imported dancing instructors to teach Japanese ladies how to sway to Western dance music. In turn, the Japanese looked down upon other "races," within their own country and outside, as inferior. One might easily speak of identification with the aggressor in the service of becoming civilized. Thus, the Japanese, now seeing themselves as civilized, mocked the "barbaric" Chinese during the Sino-Japanese War and described Russia as an "uncivilised country still sunk in barbarism" just before the Russo-Japanese war.[10] Japan had joined the community of civilization, it would appear, with a vengeance.

Put more favorably, one might use one of the terms mentioned earlier, "acculturation" or "accivilization," to describe Japan's encounter with civilization and its contents. It is, in fact, a signal example of the porosity of the notion of civilization and the striking openness of Japan to what was outside itself. Of course, we must not get carried away. Post-Meiji Japan was selective as to what it took in, and in the debates on civilization, care was taken to try to preserve what was "distinctively" Japanese. Although willing to absorb large amounts of outside culture, the Japanese were hostile to the idea of immigrants. Racial purity was to be preserved. As one thinker, Kawakatsu Heita argued, or so we are told, Japan should "limit the entry of foreign workers and instead promote overseas investment," thus assisting other peoples to exist in their native habitat.[11] This piece of self-interested casuistry could not have been put better by any spokesman for European civilization.

Overall, Japan can be said to have subjugated its own civilization, assuming we can use that term to describe its pre-Perry society, in order to become part of European civilization with its claim to being worldwide and universal. As we have seen, however, the reality of the latter was often far from this ideal. In the process, like the Egyptian and other ancient civilizations brought

back to life by the Europeans, Japan seems to have been incorporated into European civilization, rather than changing it signifi-
cantly or being seen as a separate and equal form of the civilizing
process.

6

A few variations on the Japanese theme are in order, for, as remarked earlier, it is prototypical of many experiences in the late
nineteenth and early twentieth centuries when Europe encountered other civilizations and they encountered the European
model. In the case of China, we have already noted that at the
time of Macartney's embassy at the end of the eighteenth century, its "civilization" was still in a position of superiority in regard to the European; or at least the Chinese saw it that way. A
Chinese civilization, in their view, had existed for millennia,
based on the dominance of the Han tribes in a basically fixed territory. However, as one scholar puts it, although "invaded time
and again by nomadic peoples . . . it had never confronted another people that represented a real threat to its civilization."[12]

In Chinese eyes, China was the only civilization under
Heaven, thus distinguishing its empire as the Middle Kingdom
(*zhongguo*). Its moral superiority was represented by the Confucian teachings, which could be studied and learned by others.
Thus, as one scholar tells us, "This Chinese-Confucian consciousness of superiority was therefore not ethnocentric in character but culturalistic, which means it was assumed to be possible
for foreigners to accept the ways of human and societal perfecti-
bility that were handed down within the 'School of Literati.'"[13]
This, in short, echoing one part of the European version of civilization and its possibilities for others, was the Chinese version of
accivilization: you can become like us.[14]

In the face of late nineteenth-century European civilization and its copying by the Japanese, China's civilization and its claims to superiority simply "declined," or rather crumbled. The Chinese had been humiliated and had begun to recognize their inferiority. The necessity of adapting and copying was evident. That adaptation was longer and later than that of the Japanese, who were the prime intermediaries. For centuries, China had been superior to Japan and its mentor in culture. Now it was China that became the pupil. Half a century after the Japanese, the Chinese acquired words for "civilization" and began the slow adaptation of China's institutions and ideas to the European challenge. A low point was the defeat in the Sino-Japanese War; Japan as a newly civilized and imperialist power on the Western model now took on the role of teacher of civilization.

The Chinese debates were similar to those of the Japanese before them. Could one take the material aspects of European civilization without the intellectual ones? Was one's whole past to be rejected as barbaric and, for example, Confucianism to be discarded? What remained, then, that was Chinese? Without going into details, we can note that China tried first to adapt to European civilization by copying its nationalism—one thinks of Sun Yat-Sen—and its penchant for some form of republican government, and then by becoming Marxist, in its Maoist form, and seeking to modernize under socialism/communism. Finally, without abandoning its communist trappings, China under Deng Xiaoping and his successors has been pursuing its own amalgamation of socialism, Confucianism, and capitalism in a unique blend.

Japan attempted to take on European civilization when the latter was in its assertive heyday. When the Chinese made the attempt, that civilization had endangered its own existence in

World War I and lost much of its self-confidence. Marxism, of course, was a part of early twentieth-century European civilization. Thus, while the Chinese process of accivilization had many features in common with the Japanese, it occurred later, facing a changed Western model, and represents a significant variation on the themes that I have been describing.

7

Thailand represents yet another variation. Confronted with European civilization in the mid nineteenth century, it responded by seeking to retain its independence by granting the minimum preconditions of colonization to satisfy the Europeans. To avoid the stigma of inferiority, the Thais went in quest of *siwilai*, a term transliterated from the English word "civilized," which they endowed with their own qualities. Retaining their own belief in Buddhism, and rejecting the identification of civilization with Christianity, the Thais initially admitted that, as their King Mongkut (r. 1851–68) put it, they were half-civilized and half-barbarian. The task, then, was to embrace *siwilai*, namely, in the form of refined manners and etiquette, and also *charoen*, meaning material progress and technological advance.[15]

In the process, they went through the same struggles as Europe itself had in its coming to modernity (cf. the battle of the ancients and the moderns in the late seventeenth century), and as its counterparts, such as Japan and even China, had in the late nineteenth century, in the development that eventuated in the concept of civilization. In earlier centuries, Thailand had recognized India and China as the centers of the world, and its own rather subordinate position in this cosmos. When in the mid nineteenth century, India and China were both defeated by the Europeans, Thailand reconfigured its conception of the world, both spatially and ideologically. In the place of a cosmos, Thong-chai Winichakul argues, Thais now saw civilization.

Now the task was to keep up with the world and find its own place in the panorama of civilization. For Westerners, this attempt is symbolized by the play/musical/film *The King and I.* As a drama, it confirms, consciously or unconsciously, the Western sense of superiority.[16] Thais are more likely to think of museums and exhibitions, rather than the play, as confirming their position among the world's civilizations. Whether the world agreed or not, this was the Thais' self-image, guaranteed to them by the notion of *siwilai.* In their translation of the term "civilization," it was not the Europeans who incorporated the Thais, but the Thais who incorporated the Europeans and thus became their equals and perhaps, in their own minds, their superiors.

8

Once the notion of civilization emerged, then, as we have seen, "lost civilizations" could also be found. The list eventually became very long: Egyptian, Mesopotamian, Kymerian, Aztec, Mayan, and numerous others, dating from different past times, were dug up and reconstructed. In another direction, mythical civilizations were conjured up—the lost civilization of Atlantis, for example—and new ones eventually imagined in the genre of science fiction. All of them carried the message of decline and fall: that once-proud civilizations were now in ruins. Look upon your own "future" was the latent warning that they brought to the modern civilization unearthing or imagining them.

These fallen civilizations also shed light on the nature of civilization itself, and represented stages in the shift from nomadic and barbarian societies to settled, agricultural ones. In this light, they tended to confirm the superiority of modern European civilization. The idea of progress, however, was shadowed by the sense of doom, as I have noted. Bourgeois nineteenth-century Europeans were not only supposedly digging their own society's grave, in the shape of communism, but also, in the shape of civilization, confirming its own end. Thus, ambivalence, conscious and unconscious, marked the European confrontation with past civilizations.

The example I have chosen is ancient Egypt. Here was a civilization that flourished for over three thousand years, with an identifiable "look," based on material objects, excavated from sites of death—the tombs—rather than from the remains of life, for example, marketplaces. I should also add here that the stone, alabaster, and other materials used were related to the geological structure of the country—its resources—or obtained by trade, subjects on which I have not really touched. It is the ancient Egyptian "spirit," carefully attuned to death and the afterworld, that has mostly figured in my account.

While, in fact, the manifestations of that spirit changed over time, and are often preserved for us in misleading remains—as with the Greeks, we see the Egyptians in their statues as people bleached of color, although originally the statues were often, for example, gaudy blues, greens, and purples—we recognize in the hieroglyphics, the flat-facing bodies, the stylized heads of kings, the sphinxlike creatures in the sands, the huge temples and their columns, and, above all, the tombs and mummies the marks of a distinct and cohesive civilization.

And like Shelley's lament, provoked by the ruined statue of Ozymandias, we recognize the signs of a vain pretension to everlasting rule and domination. That great civilization is no more. We know it only in the objects excavated by imperialist spades, and their resurrection by the archaeologists and linguists working from the end of the eighteenth century until the present. In itself that civilization certainly no longer exists in twenty-first-century Egypt. If the latter can claim a form of civilization, it is in terms of somehow belonging to something we now call modern civilization. In this sense, it is more like Japan, China, Thailand, and other countries that we might have considered, an-"other" civilization going through the process of accivilization.

In selecting Japan as my contemporary prototype for that process, I have deliberately chosen an-"other" civilization that, in order to preserve "itself," deliberately opened itself in an extraordinary degree to the threats and promises of European civilization. In doing so, Japan has become a foremost carrier of the civilizing process of the human species as it moves, for better or for worse, in a global direction. China, with a much greater past civilization, has been later, slower, and more ambivalent as to the contents of the Western civilization forcing itself upon it. Thailand has been yet another variation on the general theme, placing its own sign of *siwilai* on the process.

It should be noted, in passing, that as part of their current accivilization, these other civilizations have taken over their own pasts. It is now their own archaeologists who dig up evidence of their past greatness. It is now in their own museums that newly found artifacts and art objects are placed. In this form, the past civilization becomes part of the aspiration to present greatness and pride. The lessons of European civilization have been taken to heart. In this sense, European civilization has lost its claim to superiority—it no longer controls the past—and it and the "other" civilizations face a common task of (1) entering into dialogue with one another, and (2) possibly constructing a new version of civilization, a global one.

6

The Dialogue of Civilizations
in a Global Epoch

1

If a civilization assumes that it is superior and, indeed, without peers, there is little likelihood that it will wish to enter into dialogue with other societies that pretend to equal status. Thus, China until the nineteenth century had no need or desire to compare itself with societies that it did not recognize as equivalent. Medieval Islam, after the twelfth century, appears to have taken a similar attitude: although it took account of the civilizations of China and India, it was mainly concerned with its own civilization and saw little reason to enter into discourse with others. Europe, as we have seen, by the nineteenth and twentieth centuries saw its civilization as incomparable because of racial superiority, which it added to the Christian basis of its self-conception. In this mode, it was prepared to talk to others, but hardly in a spirit of equality.

In fact, Europe's sense of superiority had taken on additional force in the nineteenth century, according to Michael Adas in his book *Machines as the Measure of Men*. At that time, he argues, while the emphasis on spiritual, or religious, superiority continued (to which I have added racial superiority), it was gradually overtaken by an emphasis on scientific and technological supremacy.[1] In this version of things, one is civilized, not only in terms of the elder Mirabeau's original definition, but in accordance with the level of one's material and economic strength. The West's primacy in this regard was made manifest in its imperialistic reach to the far corners of the globe.

Yet European civilization, by virtue of its expansionism, and of its core values of science and trade, needed to know about "others." Thus, as we have seen, it deciphered the Rosetta Stone and resurrected ancient Egyptian civilization. It challenged other contenders to civilization, such as Japan, China, and Thailand, the particular examples I have chosen to stand for a host of cases, to give up their own versions and to take on the trappings, if not the convictions, of the European model, now seen as worldwide. In short, European civilization was curious about others out of both self-interest and a dedication to knowledge for its own sake.

Moreover, as we have noted, European civilization was also racked by self-doubt. For example, the famed fin de siècle is filled with foreboding and a sense of doom. Joseph Conrad peered into the "heart of darkness" in an Africa where barbarism overwhelms the rationality of Western man. Bram Stoker's *Dracula* (1897) had that darkness penetrate into the heart of England itself. In Vienna, as the nineteenth century ends, Sigmund Freud had descended into the underground caverns of the mind, showing how thin the veneer of civilization covering man's vaunted rationality is. And thus Europe's superiority.

Out of this combination of factors, Europe became "open" to others to an extraordinary degree (which does not mean that it abandoned its basic sense of superiority). Unsure of what civilization really meant, of where its future lay, in this mood, Europe

played with a belief in pluralism. Coupled to its feelings of inse-
curity, this belief was supported by a strong anthropological
sense, which "objectively" recognized "others" and their civilization. Going back, for example, to Forster in the eighteenth century, and taking on disciplinary form in the nineteenth, anthropology and its sister study sociology loosened European civilization's simple view of itself as "it." In principle, then, Europe was
now prepared to talk with others.

In practice, of course, European civilization had been imposing itself and its terms on all others. The recent history of the latter, in turn, had become a matter centrally of their coming to
terms with *that* civilization as the carrier of modernity. It is a
struggle continuing all over the globe today. Against this background, a call went out at the end of the millennium from a
number of non-Western quarters, although mainly the Middle
East, for a "dialogue of civilizations." This call took on global
features in the form of a UN declaration that made the year 2001
the year of the "Dialogue of Civilizations." I shall look at the
dialogue in detail as one of the two parts that follow in this
chapter.

The other part will take up the question of whether, transcending the dialogue, a new, global civilization is emerging. This
will involve me in a brief analysis of what is meant by globalization, how it can be viewed in historical perspective, and how it is
related to the dialogue of civilizations. In short, although each has
independent importance, I want to treat the dialogue and the possibility of a global civilization as connected topics.

2

Today's call for a dialogue of civilizations is multivoiced. For example, a few years ago, a Malaysian philosopher and activist,

Chandra Muzaffar, founded a Center for Civilizational Dialogue
at the University of Malaysia. A year or so earlier, Farouk al-
Shara, the foreign minister of Syria, with then Prime Minister
Ehud Barak of Israel at his side, welcomed the idea of an end to
violence and held out the prospect that such a move would
"usher in a dialogue of civilization and honorable competition in
various domains—the political, cultural, scientific and economic."[2] Unquestionably, however, the leading spokesman in this regard has been President Muhammad Khatami of Iran.

A major stimulus for the call to dialogue has been Samuel
Huntington's *The Clash of Civilizations* (1996). Its importance is
in inverse proportion to its scholarly worth, but that is often the
case with an argument that catches the public mood. With the
Cold War over in the early 1990s, a powerful need was felt in
some quarters for a substitute enemy that would allow for a
black-and-white conflict such as existed in relation to communism. Islam, of which he knew little, was seized upon by Huntington. Borrowing the phrase "clash of civilization" from the distinguished Islamicist Bernard Lewis, Huntington treated the
Muslim world and its belief systems as more or less a monolith.[3]

A topic of peripheral interest in America, and that mainly
among scholars and some policy makers, the notion of a clash of
civilization was like a red flag in the Arab world. Some responded
by seizing the flag under which to mobilize their struggle. Thus,
we are told, a Hamas fighter in Gaza proclaimed that "ours is not
just a struggle for land. It is a struggle of civilisation."[4] This view
seemed to echo the inadvertently expressed gut reaction of the
American president, who, in the immediate aftermath of September 11, proclaimed a "crusade," in the name of Western civilization, a proclamation that he subsequently had to tone down.
The Iranian president, Khatami, with Huntington directly in

mind, inveighed against those who "want to stir negative feelings against the West in the Muslim world and against Muslims in the West," and ended by declaring that "we must strongly prevent a clash among civilizations and religions and the spread of hatred."[5] "Civilization" is clearly a fighting word, a serious political matter.

I want to focus on the dialogue and what it means. The starting point is to recognize that the clash is fundamentally not between but within civilizations. It is both political and cultural, in the sense that those calling for a dialogue are usually reformers who want selectively to open their "civilization" to the West, while reaffirming their own cultural traditions. While made global by the UN call in 2001, the subject of dialogue is a litmus issue for Islamic regimes, and especially for Iran. In seeking to understand this situation, our task is complicated by the fact that we are forced to deal at one and the same time with the Arab world as a whole—a vastly differentiated and complicated entity—with Islam, and with Iran. While there is much overlap, distinctions must also be made. Our task is made especially difficult because of the contentious political nature of the subject.

3

Although I shall concentrate on Iran as we try further to understand some of the contemporary contents of "civilization," it is useful to look first at Arab civilization as an entity. This is comparable to talking about European civilization. The Arabic word for civilization as given in the *Oxford Arabic Dictionary* is either *madaniyya*, which comes from *madina*, or city, and thus equates civilization with the polis; or *hadara*, which conveys the idea of sedentariness versus nomadism; or *tammadun*, which also comes from *madina* and conveys a sense of refinement and cultivation, along with urbanity. There is also the term *umrân*, used by Ibn Khaldun.[6]

The beginnings of Arab civilization are linked to the coming of Muhammad as the Prophet of Islam. In the seventh century A.D., his revelation sparked the shift from nomadic tribesmen to urbanites as the core of Arab society, not all at once but certainly over time and as basically conceived. This is evident in Muhammad's move into Yathrib, a city north of Mecca, and his change of its name to Medina, which "means city and from which the term civilization *[tammadun]* is derived." As Mehdi Mozaffari argues, for example, from the beginning the Prophet aimed at a universal religion with a universal message, the carrier of a new civilization. This civilization was embodied in an empire, spread by the force of arms, and also by proselytizing and pedagogy. In the words of Arnold Toynbee, "Muslim civilization began only when Islamic schools spread through the *Umma* or community of the faithful, from the Atlantic to the Pamirs."[7]

The spread of Islam was extraordinarily rapid and far-reaching. By the twelfth century, it stretched, as indicated, over a large portion of the known world and threatened Europe. It was rich and cultivated, far advanced over its neighbors to the north, possessing the classics of the Greeks as well as its own opulent literature. It is at this point, in the eyes of many scholars, that it turned inward and became dogmatic. Emphasizing that Islam was perfect, and that, in Mozaffari's words, "Medina with its fixed set of values (unchanged for ever) is perceived as the Perfect City, the sublime form of human organization and the unique valid model for humankind," it saw no reason to be interested in others. These could generally be regarded as barbarians.[8] Arabic civilization in the Middle Ages was held as dominant, with nothing to be gained from other forms of civilization (except perhaps through selective incorporation by slavery and raw materials). Islam in the twelfth century, in its assertion of superiority, was the counterpart of Europe in the nineteenth century, with religion rather than race as the defining feature.

Summarizing what this civilization consisted of, Aziz al-Azmeh declares: "By Arabic civilization in the Middle Ages I intend the vigorous, triumphant and triumphalist ecumenical culture of Arabic expression which was embraced by peoples of different native languages and varying religious traditions across a vast area, unified by trading and currency networks, by a uniform political culture expressed in palatine and administrative norms, iconographies, representations, and enunciations of power, and by a vigorous class of traders and scholars."[9] Specific in its application, the above also offers us a definition of civilization with universal claims. It is Arab civilization so defined that claimed a temporal and cultural centrality, that is, constituted itself as civilization *toute complète* in its most confident moments.

As we can see, like other civilizations before and after it, the Arab established its own identity by distinguishing itself from the barbarians without. It saw itself as citified, polished, and refined. Its self-image was as a society and culture superior to any other. It fulfilled the definition of a dominant civilization given in our first chapter, as made up of two parts: an explicit world vision, in this case mainly expressed in religious terms, and an empire, represented by a coherent political, military, and economic system. In its vision, there was no or little room for accivilization, which could only mean decline and fall from a perfect state.

The contest with European civilization was for a long time in the favor of the Arabs. As late as the seventeenth century, Islam was pounding at the gates of Vienna. Thereafter, the tide turned. I have already remarked upon Napoleon's invasion of Egypt in connection with the Rosetta Stone and the recovery/discovery of ancient Egyptian civilization. The French invasion also heralded the decline of existing Arabic civilization and its claims to power. That shock has spread over the course of two centuries, with Islam on the defensive and the Arab world increasingly filled with a sense of humiliation. It is into this situation, so briefly sketched, that we must now place our discussion of the current call for a dialogue of civilizations.

4

In dealing with our chosen example, Iran, we are immediately faced with a problem. Is it part of Arab civilization or of something called Persian civilization? And where in this question do we fit the notion of Islamic civilization? The answer seems to be that the issue is contested. Iranians are not Arabs, nor do they speak Arabic (their language is Farsi). When the last shah, Mohammad Reza Pahlavi, wished to celebrate his reign, he harked back to a glorious Persian past two thousand five hundred years ago, and erected his pavilions in Persopolis. Yet his immediate policy was to make Iran a nation-state, modeled on those of the West. When he was overthrown in 1979, it was still in the name of an Iranian revolution. Within a short time, this revolution was turned into an Islamic revolution with universal claims and aspirations by Ayatollah Khomeini.

At this point, Iran seems to join itself to the Arab world, submerging much of its past in a common Islamic civilization. Yet that past still clings to it, and when President Khatami speaks of a "dialogue among civilizations," we are told, he uses the Persian expression *goftegu-ye tamaddon-ha*.[10] The civilization he has in mind appears to be specifically Iranian. Yet, as we have seen, that same call for dialogue has also been made in the name of an Arab

state—Syria—and an Islamic one, Malaysia. Thus, the interlocutors in what is generally called the "Middle East" (although
Malaysia can scarcely be included in that area) are varied as well
as overlapping and interlocking.

Having flagged the enormous complications involved—and I
haven't even mentioned the Shiite-Sunni division within Islam—
I want to focus on Khatami's call. As is well known, since the
death of Ayatollah Khomeini, the Iranian/Islamic revolution has
settled into a struggle between hard-liners and reformers. The
former claim that power belongs to the clerics, with no separation
between religion and the state. The latter, while still wishing for
an Islamic state, embrace a more democratic version. Ironically,
the support for the reformers comes mainly from a newly educated and literate youth, fostered and trained by the hard-liners
themselves. The contest is, of course, political as much as religious. A central battle seems to be over relations with the West,
and the question of how to adjust to the challenge of modern
civilization. The Islamic perfectionists—Islam is all-perfect and
has nothing to gain from others—wish no contact, while the reformers are open to dialogue and thus possible accivilization.

Khatami, a minor cleric, scholar, and librarian—before becoming president in 1997, he was head of the National Library—
who lived briefly in Germany in 1978, had written on comparative civilization as early as 1993, in his book of essays *Fear of the
Wave*. In one of these essays, "Our Revolution and the Future of
Islam," his first words are "Civilizations rise and fall."[11] At its ze-
nith, however, he points out, Islam acted as the conduit between
all ancient civilizations, which ranged from the Sumerian to the
Roman, and the modern age. Today, he acknowledges, Western
civilization reigns supreme; but the implication is, of course, that

it too will fall. Meanwhile, there is interplay among civilizations, as there has been in the past.

Khatami emphasizes two fundamental factors in the rise and fall of civilizations: "the dynamism of the human mind and the concomitant surfacing of new needs and necessities in human life." Every civilization, he continues, "is based on a specific worldview which is itself shaped by a people's idiosyncratic historical experience." When this synthesis is outgrown by a people's real situation, it must turn "to other civilizations for clues." In this turn, however, the old and the new clash, as "the previous civilization will not easily relinquish its entrenched and institutionalized dominance."[12] Whether intentionally or not, Khatami drew the lines of the future struggle between hard-liners and reformers that broke out in 1997.

Without going into great detail, the rest of Khatami's article sees the West as "old and worn out," racked by crises, and still wedded to colonialism in a new form, but nonetheless controlling the global economy. As much as Islamic civilization, it is necessarily on the verge of change. Khatami is appreciative of the way the West has freed humans from the shackles of many oppressive traditions and promoted the idea of liberty and freedom. The Islamic religion, however, like all religions, "sheds light on questions of eternity, charting a general and timeless path for humanity," and, Khatami implies, in this regard Islam is both more advanced than the West and potentially perfect. Yet in its earthly manifestations, it can become outdated, and he points out that a person who lived in the second or third Islamic centuries, for example, could not "solve even the smallest of today's problems."[13]

I have quoted enough from this article, I hope, to show how complex and convoluted Khatami's position is and how much

would have to enter into a dialogue of civilizations as he con-
ceives it. Much of what he says reflects the tortured political
situation of post-Khomeini Iran. Khatami and the reformers are
obviously positioning themselves in the struggle for power
around the notion of a dialogue of civilizations. Nevertheless, the
bottom line is that Khatami believes that Iran must enter into
contact with the West—as he remarked in his inaugural speech as
president, "in our world, dialogue among civilizations is an ab-
solute imperative"—and believes that in the process Iran can
hold on to its Islamic soul.[14] His hard-line opponents lack that
confidence.

   In the 1993 article, Khatami declared that Iran will be the seat
of a "new civilization," which is "on the verge of emergence." In
another article, he recognizes that "inquiry into the nature of the
information world is inseparable from uncovering the nature of
modern civilization itself."[15] But then, in postmodern style, he
reminds us that one must accept science but need not accept the
social context in which it may accidentally (as he sees it) be embedded. He is clearly "open" to new ideas. Indeed, in a long article written in 1998 for a German newspaper, he argued that tradition needs to be critically analyzed; but so, he claims, do the
notions of modernity and development. It is such questioning,
on the part of both the West and Islam, that will make possible
the emergence of a new civilization. Religion may be eternal, but
it is in the nature of civilizations to change, and we are on the
verge of just such a major transformation.[16]

5

I want to conclude my discussion of Khatami and his call for a
dialogue of civilization with a few specific observations on its po-

litical meaning, and then end with a more general assessment. In the Preface, I have alluded to my personal involvement with Khatami's Institute for Discourse on Civilization, and my aborted visit to Tehran. I refer there to the meeting in Berlin that resulted in the arrest of two members of the institute. In spite of such setbacks, the ramifications of the call to dialogue remain many. For example, a few years ago, the Iranian minister of culture and Islamic guidance exchanged views with the culture minister of the Vatican, and, we are told, "on the dialogu [sic] amongst civilizations," the Iranian minister noted, "Islam is the religion of dialogu and the Prophet Mohammad (peace be upon him) was famous for his great attention to the interlocutors' speeches."[17] The resolution presented to the United Nations calling for the year 2001 to be designated as the year of dialogue received widespread support from the Muslim nations of Asia and Africa. In short, in this view Christianity and Islam, the West and Iran, are not presumed to be in a clash but in a dialogue, blessed by the Prophet himself.

This was certainly not the view of Ayatollah Khomeini, who was notoriously uninterested in discussion and dialogue. "Politics and religion are one," he said repeatedly. And the one true religion was Islam, with nothing to learn from anyone or anything else. As he remarked during one interview, "Islam . . . contains everything . . . includes everything . . . is everything . . . perfect . . . pure."[18] Like many other clerics, he saw the West as "poisoning" Iranian youth, as harboring a "corrupt germ" that needs to be driven out of history and Iran. The implication is clear that quarantine, not dialogue, is the way to act in regard to this other civilization (if one cannot exterminate it, the ideal response).

The contrast with President Khatami and his followers is

glaring. Visiting France in 1999, Khatami laid flowers at the tomb of Emile Zola, the renowned defender of Dreyfus, a Jew falsely accused of spying (Khomeini had staged a trial of Iranian Jews accused of spying for Israel); one should note that this gesture was ignored in both the French and the Iranian media, except for one external dissident Iranian paper. In his visit to the Pantheon, Khatami also honored Rousseau, Hugo, and Marie and Pierre Curie, all iconic figures of European culture. Yet, in almost the same breath, Khatami declared that "[t]he New World Order and the globalization that certain peoples are trying to make us accept . . . in which the cultures of the entire world are ignored, looks like a kind of neocolonialism."[19]

Certain conclusions can be drawn from what has been said and quoted so far. First, the clash of civilizations is fiercest inside the Islamic civilization itself: between Khomeini and Khatami and their followers, and between those who are open to modernity and those who are closed to its siren call. Second, those who do call for a dialogue of civilizations, while open to influences from outside, do not wish to abandon their own traditions and civilization. Criticism of traditions is one thing; but it must be accompanied, they argue, by criticism of modernity as well. In taking this position, of course, the Iranians can be seen as embracing the Western modernity that is itself engaged in a criticism of its own modernity.

Yet underneath Khatami's dialogue in the name of Islam is his vague inclination to the possibility of a new civilization. The implication is that it will be some sort of amalgamation of the best of the West and Islam, but with each preserving its own identity. What it will not be is a new global civilization. With all his efforts at understanding the information revolution, Khatami had little interest in exploring its possible implications in regard to a possible global civilization. Such an exploration would be both out of his ken and of no service in his political struggles. Only a Khomeini had been interested in a global civilization, in his case, of course, a global Islamic civilization, of a religious nature.

A dialogue of civilizations assumes the continued importance of different civilizations. It does not transcend them. Religion might, but that is not Khatami's message, although it is that of Ayatollah Khomeini. For any notions about a global civilization, as transcending both a clash and a dialogue of its constituent parts, we must look elsewhere and do so more or less on our own. That is the task to which I now turn. In doing so, I add one last reminder. The content of Iran's struggle with accivilization must be viewed as one of the most recent examples of what we have already encountered in the case of Japan, China, and Thailand, which I have treated as representative of so many other societies.

6

The difficulties of dealing with the concept of global civilization are manifest and daunting. Like the notion of civilization, globalization is diffuse and highly contested. The combination of civilization and globalization is awesome. At a minimum, perhaps, we can start by thinking of globalization as a process or set of processes that transcends existing boundaries of states and societies. So defined, globalization has taken place in many guises, such as the plagues and migrations studied by scholars in world history, and at many moments in the past. Extending the definition to its furthest reaches, we can say that *Homo sapiens* has been engaged in a sort of globalization during its entire existence as a hunter-gatherer species wandering across the world. In that mode, of course, humanity had not yet turned to settled life, and its global experience could have no possible connection to civilization.

The globalization in which we are presently interested, however, although it had deep roots in the past, primarily involves what has been occurring since the second half of the twentieth century. For many scholars, it is mainly an economic process; and there are heated arguments about whether there is anything really new today or whether there was even greater per capita investment, and so on, globally, in the late nineteenth century, mainly by Great Britain. This seems to me an extremely narrow take on the subject. An enlarged definition of what is involved in globalization is needed; and it can only be supplied by an interdisciplinary perspective, with history at its core. Such a definition is a prerequisite, obviously, for any discussion of the possibility of a global civilization

A new subfield, new global history, has arisen to help supply the desired enlarged definition. It focuses on a number of new factors and takes as its starting point certain basic facts of our time: our thrust into space, imposing upon us an increasing sense of being in one world—Spaceship Earth—as seen from outside the earth's atmosphere; satellites in outer space that link the peoples of the earth in an unprecedented fashion; nuclear threats in the form of either weapons or utility plants, showing how the territorial state can no longer adequately protect its citizens from either military or ecologically related "invasions"; environmental problems that refuse to conform to lines drawn on a map; and multinational corporations that increasingly dominate our economic lives.[20]

Other factors can be noted, ranging from human rights to world music. Even with an incomplete list, however, it should be clear that something new emerged in the second half of the twentieth century. The step out into space is a truly revolutionary, or rather an evolutionary, step of monumental significance (not yet sufficiently appreciated), in the condition of humanity. The satellites have made for an enormous compression of space and time (naturally with earlier steps leading to it), and, with the computer, have contributed to an information revolution. This development, in turn, is linked to cultural developments whose consequences are not yet clear. What should be clear, however, is how limited a purely neoclassical economic approach to globalization is (although it grasps at one part of the phenomena). Indeed, if I had to sum up the core meaning in the present process of globalization, I would declare it to be a profound change in consciousness, rooted in material and institutional transformations.

Research into these matters in empirical and theoretical terms is only at an early stage. (For details of the New Global History Initiative, see www.newglobalhistory.org.) Opinions and judgments about globalization, pro and con, are widespread, with evaluation running far ahead of comprehension based on the sort of scholarship that can legitimately be expected in regard to other, similar topics. All of which makes the first term in our inquiry regarding the possible emergence of a global civilization especially unsettled. With this understood, however, we can forge ahead with our attempt. As further work of a solid nature is done on the globalization of our times, which itself, of course, is constantly in process of changing, what follows will have to be stringently reviewed and rewritten.

7

Having touched on the pitfalls concerning our understanding of present-day globalization, I now need to issue a reminder of the difficulties we have had in dealing with the subject of civilization and its previous contents. A further caution is in order: the very definition of civilization, evolved over millennia, may have to be seriously revised in any discussion of the possibility of a global civilization. One quick example can show why: where are the barbarians, or others, in a civilization experienced by all of humanity? Beyond even this caution, we must envision the possibility that the concept "civilization" has reached the limit of its usefulness and should be discarded (in the next and last chapter, I shall examine this suggestion).

Tentatively trying out our wings, however, let us attempt to touch briefly on some of the issues, emphasizing the civilization aspect of the global civilization equation. Let us recall some of our earlier definitions, or conditions, of civilization. In its origins, what we now call civilization arose on the heels of a profound climate change, leading hunter-gatherers to settle in fixed abodes and to raise crops and domesticate other animals. With this step, about 12,000 years ago, societies arose with larger populations, surplus production, social stratification, division of labor, and striking intellectual and material changes, such as priestly religions and technical innovations of various sorts. The civilizations that resulted seem to have had had an inherent dynamism, leading to growth, extension, and then decline and fall. (Another way of looking at this dynamism might be to view it as a process of accivilization.) Although *Homo sapiens* seems to have originated in Africa, the developments listed above were mainly in what has come to be called the Fertile Crescent, or the Middle East.

I am not, however, trying to write a prehistory of civilization. Nor, indeed, even a history of civilization. Our concern is with thinking about the contents of the subject, noting as we have that the reification of the term was a relatively recent development, at the hands of Victor Riqueti Mirabeau in the eighteenth century. It is the consequent spread and further elaboration of the neologism that has engaged our attention. We have looked at civilization as an ideology, benign as well as racist in its ideological expression, and at the impact of the European version on non-Western civilizations. It is in this context that the call for a dialogue of civilizations must be considered, and along with it the notion of a global civilization.

Standing back from the subject, as I noted in Chapter 1, a central definition of civilization is that it is a "junction between a world vision and a historical formation." Or, as another scholar puts it, civilization can be described as "corresponding between material conditions of existence and inter-subjective meanings."[21] Can such a definition inform our consideration of global civilization, or does it make for a poor fit? While we can probably work well with the material conditions of existence, what is the world vision behind globalization? And in what sense is globalization a historical formation, that is, "a coherent political, military and economic system usually concretized as an empire," as earlier we saw Mehdi Mozaffari define it? These are questions we must keep in mind as we try to strike out afresh in regard to a possible global civilization.

For example, Octavio Paz, soaring high above the details, announces: "The old plurality of cultures, postulating various and contrary ideals, and offering various and contrary views of the future, has been replaced by a single civilization and a single future. . . . All of today's civilizations derive from that of the Western world, which has assimilated or crushed its rivals. . . . World history has become everyone's task."[22] As we have seen, Iranians, such as Khatami, might agree with the last part of Paz's statement, but hardly with the first. Ironically, Khomeini would agree with both parts, but his single civilization would be that of Islam, not some Western-derived global construct.

In a more scholarly fashion, Almut Höfert and Armando Salvatore argue that "as a systematically compelling stage in the global civilizing process," modernity is, in fact, bringing about a situation in which there are no longer separate civilizations in the twenty-first century.

Even religion has become a generic category since the Enlightenment, in which there is a "single essence common to all religions."[23] The implication is that religion no longer truly differentiates among civilizations but can and does exist as an essence in a common civilization.

In an even more affirmative mode, some scholars argue for a global civilization. In this view, we need to think in terms of a global civilization and local cultures (the title, incidentally, of one of the early conferences of the New Global History Initiative).[24] In this picture, we can take the position that, until the twenty-first century, what were previous civilizations—the Chinese, the Iranian, and so on—can today more profitably be viewed as cultures. As such they have a semi-autonomous existence, but only as part of a larger, shared civilization.

This is the position I think can be most usefully pursued as we contemplate the possibility of a global civilization. Such a civilization can be said to have a common basis in science and technology, which, whatever their local coloring, have universalistic qualities: for example, physics and its findings are the same in China as in the United States; so, too, an automobile functions in the same mechanical manner in both societies. All peoples in the twenty-first century, therefore, live in the same "sci-tech" civilization, a term I use in imitation of the sci-fi civilizations projected as variations on what I am calling the sci-tech theme. Needless to say, they do not live in it in equal degrees or in a completely uniform manner. Sci-tech is always received or practiced in local cultural terms.

There is no center, or territory in the traditional sense, in this sci-tech civilization. As a result of the information technology revolution, we live in a networked society, which implies living in a virtual space. This does not mean doing away with local place. Or with bonds other than to humanity at large: tribal, regional, and national ties will persist. The global is only an additional bond, made possible by the factors that I listed earlier as defining present-day globalization. Among them, to repeat, are the step into space and a new view of ourselves, along with the satellite communication systems, which in turn make possible the spread of multinational economic activity, which in turn facilitates a common, although not homogeneous, cultural achievement.

The global civilization that results from all these factors and others is a process only now coming into being, and whose dimensions are still highly controversial. Is place really being supplanted by space? The question, I believe, is badly phrased: rather it should be, what are the ways in which space is newly relating to place? The same applies to the binary of homogenization versus heterogeneity, and the role of the multinationals in achieving the former. The question is in what ways homogenization is taking place, and ditto for heterogeneity, not whether one of them is sweeping the other away. Indeed, I am tempted when faced with a binary statement in regard to globalization to reach immediately for my red pen.

It must be recognized, however, that what may be greeted with warm acceptance by some—say, sci-tech as the basis for a global civilization—may be regarded with great suspicion and rejected by others. This is part of a centuries-long debate over modernity and mechanization, only expressed in contemporary idioms. The same Albert Einstein, dismissed by Hitler as practicing "Jewish science," while convinced of the universality of his physical theories, was nonetheless skeptical about the technology to which science was applied. In the shadow of World War I, he remarked that "our entire much-praised technological progress *and civilization generally* [emphasis added], could be compared to an axe in the hand of a pathological criminal."[25] Not surprisingly, we hear echoes of this view in Einstein's epistolary exchanges with Sigmund Freud.

Politicians are frequently even more dismissive than Einstein, the scientist. Thus, Václav Havel, the playwright and former president of Czechoslovakia, is unhappy with science in general, and especially its material embodiments, and denounces "the global automatism of technological civilization," which he equates with "the soulless 'automatism' of Soviet-type societies."[26] Mahathir bin Mohamad, the former prime minister of Malaysia, while promoting the technological development of his country, does not like the values associated with the process. Thus, he looks at the possibility of a global civilization with a very jaundiced eye, seeing it as merely a cover for the advancement of Western interests. In his words, "Everything will continue to be cooked in the West. And what is from the West is universal; other values and cultures are superfluous and unnecessary. Thus the globalized world will be totally uniform."[27]

What occasioned this last outburst was a charge against Mahathir's Malaysia for violating human rights. Are they also, along with sci-tech, a requisite part of a global civilization? While acknowledging the extremely controversial nature of this matter, I would argue that this is, indeed, so. The implementation of human rights is fostered by the informational network, located in no particular territory, and does not allow for any sort of "two culture" divide, separating science and values. It also transcends the local and particular. For Mahathir, on the contrary, there are no rights by virtue of being human; only local particular customs and definitions are acceptable. Human rights imply humanity and a global civilization.

The Western civilization, which Mahathir treats as monolithic, is itself divided on the issue. Thus, some postmodernists would support his view as to the relative nature of rights. A well-known philosopher, Charles Taylor, avers that there is no "abstract principle" of freedom, and thus of rights, but rather diverse judgments in different societies, for example, India or Iran, as to what constitutes acceptable freedom of speech. Hence in this view, their censorship of what they consider blasphemy is not a violation of an individual's rights but an assertion of cultural standards. As another scholar sums up Taylor's position, "To stand above and outside 'local conditions' with a single criterion implicitly endorses 'the superiority of the West.' "[28]

Pluralism, multiculturalism, political correctness, these phrases hang in the air surrounding the dialogue of civilizations and, of course, the question of a global civilization. It is an ongoing argument, one on which I have definite views. Here, however, I wish only to nod in recognition of the debate. Instead, I take as my present task, not to pursue that argument, but to inquire further into a few of the other possible aspects of a global civilization.

One useful topic concerns identity. Is a global identity required for a global civilization, on the model of a national identity for a nation-state? The answer is hardly simple. First of all, peoples can have multiple identities, so that within the nation-state local, regional, and national identities can coexist all at the same time. Next, individuals can form part of a nation-state without necessarily adopting its national identity, for example, Kurds in the Turkish nation-state. There is no self-evident reason, therefore, to think that peoples cannot add to this mix a global identity, or even exist in a global civilization without a conscious sense of belonging to it.

The elements making for a global identity, willy-nilly, consciously or unconsciously, are some of the following. For example, a common language, English, is shared by increasing numbers of the world's population. Even more universal is the language of mathematics, which also underlies the computer revolution. Another increasingly common language is "world music." In another dimension, the visual, films and TV, transmits shared images. For another example, a more static one, we can turn to the logo of the planet earth as viewed from outer space. So, too, food has become more widely shared across cultures, with McDonald's in Tokyo and sushi restaurants in New York. One critic has summed up this trend as leading to a McDonald world; but this is surely a one-sided view.

Mention of McDonald's can lead to a renewed look at the civilizing process, as theorized by Elias. We are told, for example, that the spread of the restaurant chain to China has resulted in a change in manners: it is no longer proper, at least in the restaurants, to spit or throw rubbish on the ground! On another tack, Stephen Mennell, perhaps the foremost Elias scholar today, reminds us that central to the civilizing process is the restraint of violence. In the late Middle Ages, this was fostered by the emerging absolutist monarchies. Can we think of the United Nations as an early stage in that same effort today? Needless to say, at the moment, it has little military force of its own, and none of the taxation that such forces need and have made possible in the past, but perhaps this will change. In any event, Elias's thesis can be extended to thinking about "the prospects for the globalization of manners" and the emergence of a global civilization. It goes without saying that this would be a "very long-term social process."[29]

Earlier, I spoke of space-time compression. In fact, the "instantaneous time" in which so much is happening is "located" in a calendric time that has become the same across the world. While particular calendars, for example, the Islamic and Japanese calendars, still persist, they do so in the context of a commonly accepted system of days, weeks, and years, as well as time zones. Thus is repeated on a global level what has occurred previously on a national level, as exemplified, for example, in the national and international adoption of standard time. The latter's connection with the coming of the railroads is matched by the present-day impact of airplanes and space travel. It is also noteworthy that air terminals are recognizably similar the world over, with architecture connecting people "spiritually" as much as the planes do spatially.

In all these ways, and many others, a global identity is coming into being. Does it amount to a historical vision? Only in an incipient fashion. Previous civilizations have shaped their vision in terms of an us and a them, the barbarians without the gates. As I remarked earlier, a networked globe ends this division. Only an imagined alien invasion from Mars or elsewhere can take its place, with humans presumably defending themselves against these new "others." Or perhaps the environment becomes the new threat from "outside"? In any case, a global civilization redefines the barbarian/civilized dichotomy, or else does away with it.

The remaining identity, if it is to exist, must be defined in new terms, presumably with its center in a shared sci-tech world and its results as hinted at above.

All in all, the notion of a center is no longer what it used to be. Previous civilizations formed around a city, or cities. These stood in vital difference to the nomadic conditions around them. Even in more recent civilizations, the now un-walled city was central to its existence. When Yeats remarked that "the centre cannot hold," metaphorically he was predicting that civilization would decline and fall. Networked society, however, does not have a center. Some critics have even argued for the end of the city as we know it, envisioning a city of bits. While this prediction probably goes much too far, it accords with a general sense that culture, and the cities in which it is "centered," have become globally diffused and decentered.

Everything I have noticed so far is controversial and a matter of a possible future as much as a present reality. Globalization is a process still in "process." Whether the outcome of this process is, or is to be, a global civilization is perhaps an even more controversial matter. The additional question of whether such a global civilization would constitute a historical vision is something we have already touched upon. Would it be a "historical system," for example, in the form of an "empire," that is, the feared American imperium, or "a coherent political, military and economic system," emerging from an international into a global form? These are posers whose answers are still unfolding. In thinking of civilization and its contents, these are issues and questions to which we have as yet no answers, but about which we can no longer avoid thinking.

8

A dialogue of civilizations presupposes the persistence of existing civilizations. While they are to remain open to the forces of ac-civilization, they retain both their autonomy and importance. Such a dialogue, moreover, serves critical political purposes in these continuing "civilizations." Clearly, the idea of a global civilization runs fundamentally counter to the dialogue notion *as it has been so far formulated*. Instead of many civilizations, in this new conception, there is conceived to be one common civilization, with numerous cultural variations. Where the two views coincide is in a call for dialogue. The difference in the second view, that of global civilization, is that it takes for granted the constituent features of globalization. Thus, it assumes a common sci-tech grounding, on whose basis a global dialogue among "cultures" may be made possible. This latter view also assumes a definite value position, however, as exemplified in the area of human rights. It is one that challenges the "closed" and "local" culture. The two views of civilization, and where it is headed, therefore point in different directions. We are, in fact, at a hinge of history, and which door we open and which vista we see beyond it have become matters of world-historical importance.

7

Conclusions

1

Has the concept "civilization" outlived its usefulness? Is it more harmful than beneficial in the effort to understand humanity and its vicissitudes? Have more evils been committed in its name than benefits visited upon mankind? Is the reality behind it a source of greater happiness or unhappiness to the species? And, finally, whatever the answers to such questions, has the content of the concept itself been hollowed out in the course of history so that only a shell of meaning is left?

Over the years, numerous books and articles have appeared with titles such as *Civilization in Crisis* or *Civilization on Trial*, or variations on that theme. These have taken the concept of civilization for granted and, generally in an agitated fashion, questioned the fate of a particular manifestation of the concept. I am suggesting that the very concept itself should be viewed as in crisis and needs now to be put on trial. Such a trial itself will be enmeshed in controversy and shrouded in the politics of our time. It is, moreover, also involved with close neighbors of the concept of civilization, such as cosmopolitanism and especially modernity. Thus, in a typical elision, Bernard Lewis speaks of Turkey as engaged in a program "to modernize, meaning to become part of modern civilization."[1] What we think of cosmopolitanism and modernity, topics deserving their own attention, although not given it here, therefore necessarily colors our views on civilization.

In pursuing my evaluation, I shall undertake to review the functions of the concept; the widespread evocation of the notion, however discredited it may be intellectually; its sibling rivalry with the idea of culture; its role in bringing happiness or unhappiness to the human species; and, finally, the future of the reification, or at least what I think its future should be. Ideally, one should approach this task as if one were an archaeologist a thousand years hence, looking at the remains of present-day civilization. In practice, I dwell among these future remains.

2

In Chapter 1, I explored the origins of the concept of civilization. As I tried to show, many factors entered into the reification taking place in the late eighteenth century. In the specific case of Victor Riqueti Mirabeau, the coiner of the neologism, one reason for his establishing the term was political: civilization became a measuring rod applied to the ancien régime. If we ask what the function of civilization is, one clear answer is that it corresponds to whatever the contemporary political needs happen to be, and that this will be true in all its manifestations.

In Chapter 1, however, my emphasis was not on the political but on the intellectual significance of the concept. As I argue there, it represented a Europe becoming self-reflective about its position in the world and history. Others will argue that this is a Eurocentric view, ignoring self-reflectivity in other societies and times. I believe that the context surrounding the European self-reflectivity sets it apart from its possible counterparts elsewhere.

The concern with social bonds was heightened at the time by the strain placed on them by the revolutionary changes, political and industrial, then occurring. One result was intense thought given increasingly to the nature of sociability, society, the public, the nation—and civilization.

In the process, greater awareness arose about the divided nature of "mankind," to use the term of the day. Humans were recognizably both altruistic and self-interested (as both Adam Smith and Immanuel Kant, for example, argued). The altruistic part of their nature led humans to cooperate and to form social groupings, ranging from the family through tribes, nations, empires, and on up to civilizations. This tendency can be seen as deeply embedded in human nature. Recent research supports this view, in fact, suggesting that humans are "wired to cooperate," that is, that there is a neural basis for our willingness to work with others and to do good deeds.[2] In addition, the struggle to survive often pushes members of the species into working together. Self-interest can then be fitted into this picture. Our own selfish ends may both be served by entering into social bonds and, as Adam Smith would have it, play a critical role in establishing such bonds.

In such a view, civilization would be the highest form of social bonding, as well as the most extensive. Thus, another function of the concept of civilization is to represent an aspiration. "The discourse of civilization in the era of nation-states is closely tied to this yearning for a transcendent spiritual purpose," as Prasenjit Duara puts it.[3] Civilization was the loftiest form in which humans could congregate, even if it was mostly spiritual and not territorial. It represented ideals of social existence for the whole of the human race.

At least it did so in this ideal conception. Perhaps more realistically, or at least as an accompaniment, it had originated as an embodiment of Europe's sense of superiority, its own sense of worth. This is a different sort of aspiration from the transcendent one. As Norbert Elias summed up this side of the matter: "The concept [of civilization] expresses the self-consciousness of the West. One could even say: the national consciousness. It sums up everything in which Western society of the last two or three centuries believes itself superior to earlier societies or 'more primitive' contemporary ones. By this term Western society seeks to describe what constitutes its special character and what it is proud of: the level of its technology, the nature of its manners, the development of its scientific knowledge of the world, and much else."[4] As we have seen, this assertion of civilization could be in the form of either a benign or a malignant "colonial" superiority.

Yet another function was to constitute social hierarchy. The concept of civilization could do this both internally and externally. Within the particular society, there could exist both those who partook of the nature of civilization and those, lesser or below, who simply did not share in its benefits. These latter were the barbarians within the gates and lower in position. Outside the particular society were to be found its inferiors in regard to civilization. To take a revealing example, on a visit to Germany, Henry Mayhew, the author in 1851 of a famous exposé of the condition of London's laboring poor, exclaimed: "How many hundred years behind us are the [German] people in all the requirements of decency and civilization, among whom such a comfortless and boorish form of existence can continue to the present day."[5] A few years later, however, the Germans were asserting *their* hierarchical superiority in regard to civilization and proclaiming themselves its foremost representatives!

In addition to a pejorative use of civilization, comparing other societies invidiously to one's own, the concept had and has another seemingly more neutral function. It can serve the purposes of social science. It represents a way of organizing history, of giving sense to the seemingly chaotic happenings of the past. A century before Darwin's theory of evolution, it could offer a proto-evolutionary explanation of how human social bonds changed shape from the hunter-gatherer stage to the nomadic, agricultural, commercial, and then civilizational stages. This stadial point of view was presented, for example, by Adam Ferguson and the Scottish Enlightenment thinkers of the late eighteenth century. It was a widely held view and was embraced by Johann Reinhold Forster, whom we encountered in Chapter 2, who remarked on "the progress of mankind from the state of brutes to that of savages; and lastly to that of civilization."[6]

Although both the idea of progress and the stadial view seem fustian today, the general concept constituted by them still is prevalent, even if often silently. There is a general sense that the mode of subsistence and of material well-being has changed and increased, at least in the parts of the world that enjoy "civilization," and that legal and political progress, for example, toward "democracy," has taken place in many parts of the world. Challenged though this view of progress may be, it seems to persist, perhaps in the new form of global civilization. Combining with the aspirations touched on earlier—the yearning for a transcendent spiritual purpose, and the attempt to express the superior self-consciousness of Europe—the social science function of the concept of civilization continues to offer some reference points for many otherwise adrift in the turbulent seas surrounding humanity's secular passage through time. Civilization thus represents a dynamic representation of a powerful binary drive in the species. The notion of "civilized" versus "barbarian," as we have noted, goes back thousands of years. It defines the us from the other in a most fundamental sense. Our binary drives are not simple: for example, some individuals, such as Rousseau, want to withdraw from society and reject civilization, thus returning to an earlier, more primitive state of lost purity. But the binary inclinations seem to be persistent, whatever their particular form. What the concept of civilization does is both embrace this binary characteristic and couple it to a sort of dialectical process.

In sum, the concept of civilization serves many functions. Many of them support and overlap with one another. Many of them conflict and contradict one another. They cluster in affinities and divide into oppositions. Together, they make up a powerful battery of reasons why the concept first came into existence and now persists in sometimes reflective and sometimes unreflective fashion. Before going on with the reflective aspect, I want to look further, even if only briefly, at its unreflective use.

3

In examining the unreflective use of the notion of civilization, we become very conscious of the dichotomy between scholarly discourse, which has become increasingly critical of the concept, and the ever-increasing invocation of it in public pronouncements. We seem, in fact, to be faced with an inverse proportion law: the less viable the concept, the more frequently it is invoked.

Let us start with the reaction to the events of September 11, 2001. The American president, George W. Bush, immediately cast the attack as one on "civilization," perceived to be embodied in the United States, and, almost as an afterthought, the West. Unthinkingly, President Bush thus at the outset embraced Huntington's "clash of civilizations" thesis. The terrorists were clearly representative of the "forces of evil," and although, to his credit, the president tried to avoid a stark identification of evil with Islam, the undertones of his remarks suggested otherwise. Such a connection was strengthened by his initial call, previously mentioned, for a "crusade," thus linking the struggle to a fateful series of medieval Christian military expeditions that targeted Islamic rule in the so-called Holy Land.

Indeed, the current use of the term "civilization" in opposition to the forces of evil echoed earlier appeals in American history, but with Germany rather than Islam as the enemy. I have before me a poster by the famous artist James Montgomery Flagg in 1917, on the eve of America's entry into World War I, portraying a sleeping young woman wearing a red-and-white-striped skirt and a star-spangled bandana. At the top, in bold letters, are the words WAKE UP, AMERICA! At the bottom it reads: CIVILIZA-TION CALLS EVERY MAN WOMAN AND CHILD![7] *Plus ça change, plus ça reste.*

Both Bush and Flagg, of course, were invoking a term, "civilization," with powerful overtones in American history. Even before the invention of the term, the idea was there in the Puritan vision of establishing a "city on a hill" (the city, of course, being the core of civilization) in a continent otherwise viewed as a howling wilderness. Almost from the beginning, however, the Americans envisioned their civilization as separate and different from the corrupt civilization of Europe from whence they had come. There were and are, of course, immense ambiguity and ambivalent feelings on the part of Americans in regard to both the "mother" countries and to civilization and its nature. Viewed on one hand with pride, civilization is seen on the other hand as a constraint on the free man, who must, like Huck Finn, constantly be lighting out for the frontier in order to avoid the spiritual and physical death of being "sivilized."

Obviously, a whole book could be written on the vicissitudes of the notion of civilization in America (courses are routinely taught in American civilization, the Beards entitled their book *American Civilization*, and there are fellowships to study the subject; these are not, however, the same as the history that I am suggesting needs writing). I have tried here, however, simply to hint at the overtones in any current invocation of the word "civilization" in the United States of America. A similar analysis would be in order for other nations and their particular employment of the term.

It is not only President Bush who speaks in the defense of civilization. The term is constantly on the tongue of the president of Russia, Vladimir Putin. In Chechnya, whose populace is mainly Muslim, it is Russian troops who are, so to speak, manning the walls against those attacking all of civilization. Time and again, Putin has used the terms "civilization" and "civilized" to describe his country. So have many of his officials. A typical example involves Kaliningrad, a part of Russia wedged between Poland and Lithuania. These two neighbors wished to end free traffic across the borders. In opposing this, the Russian director of the region said, "I cannot understand who wants this. We are not savages here. We are part of European civilization."[8]

Of course, a glance at Russian history suggests that the matter is not so simple. For centuries, harking back to the time of Peter the Great, Russia has been the scene of a conflict between Slavophiles and Westernizers. Both, of course, viewed themselves as in favor of civilization. But for the former this meant a special Russian, Orthodox Christian version; only for the latter was the desired civilization that of Europe at large. Even in Soviet times, there was great ambivalence about the concept, with its Western overtones. The entry "Tsivilizatsiia" in the Soviet *Historical Ency-*

clopedia, for example, notes that the term derives "(from the Latin *civilis*—civil, governmental)—a synonym for the concept of culture; the totality of the material and spiritual achievements of society in its historical development." Citing the use of the term by Marx and Engels as applied to "a specific state of social development succeeding wildness and barbarism," the entry also acknowledges the "origins of the concept in the French eighteenth century."[9]

So far, so good. Then, at the end, the entry concludes: "In contemporary bourgeois historiography, the concepts of civilization and the replacements of civilization are frequently opposed to Marxist teachings about the process of development and replacement of socioeconomic formations." As one expert, Loren Graham, remarks, "I have been struck by how in Soviet scholarship and writings the term [civilization] rarely occurs."[10] Thus, product though Putin is of the Soviet KGB, in using the term, he is distancing himself from that era and embracing the notion that Russia is part of European civilization. Now in the new era, the term is in constant use. We need only to remember that for those who hear it invoked in Russia, just as in the case of Bush and America, it carries a great deal of baggage.

In the cases of America and Russia I seek simply to establish a prototype of how one must invoke the past echoes in all situations where the term is used. Now I shall simply give, as testimony to its current widespread usage, a few more quotations, selected almost at random, to illustrate the omnipresent and often surprising invocation of the term. Needless to say, the political function in the examples cited generally overcomes any reflection on the term and its contents.

The most neutral example is a recent advertisement for the president of the European University Institute. The person selected is to lead the institute's training in the human and social sciences, which, along with law and economics, specifically include "History and Civilization."[11] Roughly of the same nature is this statement by the elected prime minister of Tibetan exiles: "What is important is to restore Tibetan civilization [we, in our turn, must reflect on what is involved in the restoration of a civilization]. Tibet is not simply a nation or state. It is a unique cultural and spiritual heritage. . . . Our basic objective is to preserve it in future for the benefit of all humanity, all sentient beings."[12] Akin to this sentiment is that of a letter writer who decries the deliberate destruction of the Buddha statues by the Taliban as "an affront to civilization."

Such statements are an invitation to dialogue by others and to discursive deconstruction at the hands of scholars. Perhaps the remaining two quotations I shall give need less commentary. The first is former Mayor Rudolph Giuliani's announcement that the homeless had no right to sleep in the streets of New York, saying, "Streets do not exist in civilized societies for the purpose of people sleeping there."[13] Here, of course, the word "civilized" stands in for civilization. The next citation, in some ways my favorite, comes from then President Slobodan Milosevic as he began his campaign in the year 2000 by praising his country's resilience and then adding an attack on the West. "This is the answer," he declared, "to violence and injustice, a proof of the civilizational superiority of our nation, undefeated and unconquered by evil."

Clearly, civilization and evil are, to use a cliché, in the eye of the beholder. What I have tried to do with this piecemeal presentation of recent quotations is to establish beyond a doubt that civilization is a trope filled with ambiguities, many of them of a political nature. It is often also a stand-in for the good, the true, and the beautiful, in a world where these qualities seem sadly missing, and violence increasingly threatening from both without and within. The term has, in fact, become a mantra, invoked with increasing frequency at a time when identities and meanings have become more and more fragile.

4

In Chapter 2, I wrote at some length about the different origins and meanings attached to the words "civilization" and "culture." Elsewhere I have mentioned that Norbert Elias treats the subject in some detail in his book *The Civilizing Process*. I want now to look a little more closely at the two concepts—civilization and culture—as they tango through much of history.

The task is made dauntingly difficult especially because of the shifting meaning of both terms. We have already acquired some idea of the multifaceted nature of the term "civilization." If we now focus on culture, we can see that the problem is even more complicated in regard to it. An attempt by two anthropologists to understand the meaning of culture came up with over 100 different definitions and emplotments. As the literary critic Raymond Williams remarks in his *Keywords*, where he has a long entry on culture (although not civilization, which he deals with only in conjunction with culture), "Culture is one of the two or three most complicated words in the English language."[14] The hard-pressed *Webster's New World Dictionary* comes up with eight separate definitions, the last being "the concepts, habits, skills, arts, instruments, institutions, etc. of a given people in a given period; civilization."

Acknowledging anew therefore the complications concerning the two concepts, a few observations may help further illuminate our topic. Both civilization and culture are eighteenth-century inventions describing processes that date back many millennia. If we apply the present-day meaning(s) of culture to the past, we can say that it is the older of the pair in the sense that hunter-gatherers, the state of humans for most of their prehistory, possessed what we would now call a "culture." It is only after the climate change about 12,000–10,000 years ago, the beginning of the present so-called interglacial period, that conditions were stable enough and favorable enough for sustained agriculture to arise, and with agriculture the *cultivation* of the earth. It is that cultivation that makes for the coming of civilization, with its settled cities, surpluses, labor divisions, social stratifications, and so on. Such civilizations arose at roughly the same time in China, India, and the Middle East. Thus there existed in these places both cultures and civilizations, to employ the terms anachronistically.

It is at this point that the two concepts began their love-hate relationship, all of this known to us, of course, in retrospect and reflection. Culture could be oral; civilization, on the other hand, seemed to have required writing. Culture could be a folk achievement; civilization had an affinity for civil society (linked to the city) and citizenship. Cultures tended to be particular and local; civilizations moved in the direction of expanded empires and the making of universalistic claims. In between these two ways of conceiving human bonds, one might place the pastoral, with its effort to straddle the divides between the nomadic, the agricultural, and the urban.

As soon, however, as these distinctions are made, the boundaries between the two terms, "culture" and "civilization," are breached. At the same time as they retain their asymmetry, they become synonyms. A typical example, although late in time, is Freud's comment in his *The Future of an Illusion*, "I disdain to separate culture and civilization." By human culture/civilization, he informs us, he means "all those respects in which human life has raised itself above animal conditions and in which it differs from the life of the beasts."[15] Others similarly conflate the two terms. Given such confusion about the two concepts, civilization and culture, even the formulation "global civilization and local cultures" takes on renewed uncertainty.

At this point, we need to collapse a very long story. We also need to be aware of the way reality—for there were cultures and civilizations before self-reflectivity set in—and thinking about that reality—our conceptualizations of it—operate on different levels. Only from the eighteenth century on, as we have seen, is there a convergence. Thenceforth, civilization and culture are entities to be reckoned with both empirically and theoretically, together and apart. In fact, as remarked earlier, it was within the bosom of thought about civilization that the notion of culture arose and then took on relatively independent existence. What is more, one can make the argument that by the late twentieth century, culture was taking over the content of civilization, or at least Western civilization.

Perhaps that story should begin in the nineteenth century with romanticism, which favored cultural relativism over civilization's universality. In any case, by the end of that century and the beginning of the next, the twentieth century, culture, the carrier of relativism, had also acquired a sense of the higher things in life—art, literature, and so forth—*and* the sense of defining the totality of social life, material and spiritual. In this latter situation, as the anthropologist Clifford Geertz puts it, culture is seen as a symbol system, a context in which social events, behaviors, institutions, and processes can be intelligibly—that is, thickly—described. Civilization seems to fade from the scene in this description.

By the late twentieth century in the West, culture appears also to have displaced race and even ethnicity. Multiculturalism emerges as the watchword for many postmodernists and other such schools of thought. Unlike civilizations, all cultures in this view are equal; the relativism of the romantic movement of the previous century has carried the day. To be cultured now means not to have manners and an acquaintance with Homer and Mozart, or to participate in the totality of social life, but to possess a way of life and a lifestyle shared by others of your taste and perhaps "roots."

The other development in regard to culture is its "takeover" by the forces of commerce. Here a different sort of boundary is being fused and confused. In the age of the Information Revolution and multinational corporations, the lines between commerce and culture, merchandising and entertainment have become increasingly obscured. Here, in an unexpected way, the forces of globalization join hands with the manner in which the meaning of culture has been changing. Paradoxically, this development means the return of the concept of civilization, which, ousted through one door, reenters by another, and the idea of a global civilization and local cultures can thus reappear triumphant.

From this multiplicity of meanings and historical phases, which I have tried to convey by highlighting a few parts of the story, one thing should be clear. The civilization/culture distinction is a muddle. In returning, therefore, to our primary concern with civilization and its contents, we must include this muddle as one of its contents, and be aware, to shift metaphors, of its tentacles as we press on with our inquiry, now in its final stages. It remains for us to take up anew the question posed by Freud concerning civilization and happiness/unhappiness, and then to come to some sort of conclusion about the future of civilization and its conceptualization.

5

In thinking of happiness and civilization, and whether these are incompatible states, it is important to look more closely at the term "happiness" itself. According to a number of scholars, the idea of happiness is a recent one, emerging in the same eighteenth century that produced the concept of civilization. The idea of happiness then prominently enters public awareness as evinced, for example, by the words "life, liberty and the pursuit of happiness" in the sacred writings of the American revolutionaries, and, more abstractly, in the philosophical doctrines of the utilitarians, with their advocacy of the "greatest good of the greatest number" as the means by which to reach general bliss. Indeed, Jeremy Bentham sought to give scientific form to this endeavor by constructing a "felicific calculus."

Did not people strive for happiness before the eighteenth century? Of course they did, but as an individual matter. The notion that everyone had a right to happiness was in earlier times an absurd one, simply not contemplated. That democratic aspiration had to await the arrival of such other concepts as the sovereignty of the people and the beginnings of the Industrial Revolution. The idea of happiness, therefore, is part of a complex of ideas revolving around the notion of humans living in societies with particular social bonds, which can be reordered by those same humans. Civilization, our own focus, is one of these "bonded" conceptions.

It is somewhere within this complex of ideas that we must place Freud's counterposing of civilization and happiness. As remarked, he was not a historian and paid scant attention to this dimension of the problem. His concern was with an eternal and universal condition, as he saw it. The psychological, not the his-

torical, occupied his mind. For him, it was the psychological notion—repression of instinct that is at the core of civilization (or
culture), and that produces unhappiness and discontent. In both
The Future of an Illusion and *Civilization and Its Discontents*, he
explores the dimensions of a timeless antagonism between instinctual desires and the restrictions of civilization.

Let us return to these two books, on which we have previously
touched briefly. As I have argued, *The Future of an Illusion* is basically about religion serving as an escape from reality. It is really
only tangentially that the question of civilization and happiness is
mentioned. Thus Freud says almost in passing: "We see that an
appallingly large number of men are discontented with civilization and unhappy in it."[16] The reason advanced here for this discontent is that "culture is based on compulsory labour and instinctual renunciation" and therefore evokes opposition.

A few years later, Freud returned to the topic in *Civilization
and Its Discontents*. This is a much broader and significant treatment of the problem, with religion still important, but as only
one of the ways in which humanity seeks to assuage its unhappiness. Others are art, science, drugs, yoga, and so on. They are
mere palliatives, unable to give us true relief. In desperation,
some advocate the renunciation of civilization and a return to
primitive conditions. Freud does not name him, but, of course,
Rousseau comes to mind.

It is important to remember that Freud himself is not hostile
to civilization. It incorporates reason, which he believes in
fiercely. He sees civilization as a necessary evolutionary step,
sheltering humanity from a threatening environment. It represents a cognitive mastery of nature, with mankind's growing
power substituting for the false satisfactions of religious illusion
and fantasy. Thus, in a memorable phrase, quoted earlier, Freud

speaks of man becoming a "prosthetic God." In the face of a hostile nature, man has taken on his own godlike character.

Yet even this cannot save him. It is *human* nature that makes humanity unhappy. In repressing our instinctual desires, we incur both feelings of guilt and an acute sense of discontent. Recognizing that his discussion of the sense of guilt disrupts the framework of his paper, Freud insists that "it corresponds faithfully to my intention to represent the sense of guilt as the most important problem in the development of civilization and to show that the price we pay for our advance in civilization is a loss of happiness through the heightening of the sense of guilt."[17]

In fact, Freud's attention to guilt as *the* essence of the problem is not only disruptive but inconsistent, although not contradictory, with what he had said earlier. As is well known, Freud placed sex at the heart of our instinctual lives. But he also recognized the "inclination to aggression" as an "original, self-subsisting instinctual disposition in man." As such, it conflicts with eros, the life instinct, "whose purpose is to combine single human individuals and after that families, then races, peoples and nations, into one great unity, the unity of mankind." To this list, we can add civilization. On the other side of love, however, is the aggression, the self-interest, that Freud has recognized as also rooted in human nature, that is, its instinctual life. In a quick leap, he concludes that "the meaning of the evolution of civilization is no longer obscure to us. It must represent the struggle between Eros and Death, between the instinct of life and the instinct of destruction, as it works itself out in the human species."[18]

In this formulation, we recognize our old friend, the social-unsocial nature of man, as limned by Adam Smith, Kant, and countless other thinkers of the Enlightenment. Freud's transmutation of it into a struggle between life and death, in the form of his (in)famous death instinct, does not seem to me, or most other scholars, an improvement. In spite of Freud's genius—and he was one—*Civilization and Its Discontents* goes little beyond an explanation of the latter part of the title, grounding it in psychoanalytic theory. It does not offer a great deal that helps us in understanding the first part of the title. There are flashes of brilliance—the prosthetic God, for instance—and some lovely writing, but not much beyond that. There is, however, one very important exception: a grounding of the civilizing process in a systematic exposition of how humanity has tried to repress its "base" instincts and sublimate them in a mannered and civilized existence.

As for happiness per se, Freud aside, common observation suggests that some people seem to be born "happy" and others not. Temperament, of course, can be affected by external happenings. Yet, putting the external aside, general disposition seems to be pretty steady. Scientific research into the conditions making for happiness is being done. Although I am skeptical that we shall be able meaningfully to measure happiness—Bentham's felicific calculus in new form?—others are more hopeful. Who knows, perhaps a gene for happiness will be found (there seems some reason to believe that there may be a gene for language)? Pending such findings, I myself conclude that happiness and unhappiness are best viewed as "built into" the members of the species. If this view is accepted, then these dispositions stand relatively independent of the material and ideational development of society. Happiness is not the measure of civilization.

With this said, one has to recognize the gains made in everyday civilized life. The availability of food, the absence of poverty, the ease afforded by mechanical contrivances, these are not to be sneered at. While there is no evidence that they are guarantees of happiness, they do tend to ameliorate humanity's lot. Nevertheless, we must remind ourselves that when Prometheus, according to the myth, stole fire from the heavens and gave it to man, thus providing light and heat—prerequisites for the development of culture and civilization—he did not also give them contentment. In fact, as we know from the rest of the myth, Prometheus was chained to a rock, with vultures picking at his liver, for eternity. Not exactly a happy ending.

6

At the beginning of this chapter, I raised the question of whether the concept of civilization had lost any real meaning, and whether it was now so hollowed out as to be more or less useless. Having examined its "contents" from the time of Mirabeau's formulation to the present, as well as looking at its "discontents," we are poised to seek some sort of concluding evaluation. I am also aware that the reader may choose to discard my evaluation, perhaps even angrily, but he or she will perhaps hold on, I hope, to the historical inquiry on which it is based.

There is an oft-quoted witticism to the effect that Gandhi, when asked what he thought of Western civilization, replied that he thought it would be a good idea. What is it that makes civilization, whether Western or not, in principle a good idea? The whole of this book suggests the range of answers. Civilization as a stage of development represents a process that has carried *Homo sapiens* far from his initial animal nature, turning him into a reflective and prosthetic God. Art, literature, language, writing, and the religion that Mirabeau identified as fundamental emerge as elements leading to civilization. The use of fire and heat in making utensils, artifacts, and weapons must be noted, along with the invention of ploughs and other instruments necessary for advanced agriculture. The building of walled cities, the erection of palaces and temples, and the fostering of trade also must be listed.

These are some of the beginning elements. In about ten thousand years or less, an incredible advance in control of the material world has occurred. An equally impressive advance, at least in terms of complexity, has taken place in human social life. By the twentieth century, forms of democracy are widespread, and ever-widening circles of group activity, from the family to the nation, are in existence. Conceptually, the highest pinnacle may be seen in civilization. These are hardly, it would seem, achievements to be thrown away.

In one particular sector of society, that of women, the gains seem to be particularly striking, although erratic. In almost all discussions of civilization since its conceptualization by Mirabeau, the status of women has been mooted as the measure of the level of civilization. Some, such as Kant, have assigned to the female sex the task of civilizing men. James Mill, though scornful of women in actuality and denying them the right to vote—claiming that their interests were already represented by their husbands—declared that how they were treated represented the dividing line between barbarism and civilization. His son, John Stuart Mill, although horrified by some of his father's opinions, nevertheless agreed that the status of women was the measure of civilization, and called for a domestic revolution. Both Freud and Nietzsche, although deeply suspicious of women, nevertheless recognized their critical role in civilization.

Stepping beyond the minds of men, we can see that in actual society, women's role has changed in many ways. They have gained the vote and entered the workforce outside the home in increasing numbers in the so-called developed countries. They are linked as equals with men in consumption. One commentator has sought to sum up this movement by declaring: "The modern domination of the life-world by style and civility . . . is a process of the feminization of society."[19] We need only to put together numerous other citations and quotations to make obvious the point that women have been seen widely, with whatever reservations, as the measure of civilization—and, by that measure, that their condition has improved in many parts of the world.

Summing up the drift of what I have been quoting and saying, one can conclude that civilization in many of its manifestations is a good thing. One would not lightly abandon it. Yet as we have seen, some would like to do just that. In the West itself, critical voices have been raised. Some of them have already been cited. Typical is that of Nietzsche, who described modern man as a sickly creature, whose sex and strength has been sapped in the deadly trap of civilization. Outside the West, the German philosopher's diatribe against civilization—from which he has removed God—is echoed by fundamentalist religious believers, who, rather than entering into dialogue, wish to destroy "godless" civilization in all its manifestations.

One does not have to be a Nietzsche or a fundamentalist to recognize that there are negative sides to civilization. Its repression of instinct, for example, can be a severe strain for many. It embodies a riven form of human coexistence. Objectively, at the heart of civilization lurk war and violence. From its very beginnings, thousands of years ago, civilization arose and spread by military as well as other means. Its current representatives still make war. The paradox, of course, is that civilization also represents the restraint of the violent and bellicose spirit. Such restraint, in fact, is at the heart of Elias's notion of the civilizing process.

Another disquieting fact about civilization is that it is so frequently accompanied by a decivilizing process. Whether one
thinks back to the inquisitions of Spain or the existence of slavery
in the United States, or concentrates on the Nazi eruption in the
twentieth century, such lapses into violence and the decivilizing
process must be taken into account alongside the civilizing process itself. The Taliban ignorantly attacked civilization by blasting
the ancient Buddha statues at Bamiyan to bits, but more "civilized" peoples have done similar things. Easy to forget, for example, is the destruction in the 1960s of the soul of the city of Kaliningrad (formerly Königsberg, a German place and the home of
Kant). Boring hundreds of holes in the city's thirteenth-century
castle, Soviet military engineers "packed them with dynamite and
began blasting away 700 years of history."[20] And then there is the
"benign" destruction of landmarks in cities such as New York by
commercial interests, in spite of the efforts of historical preservation societies.

Whatever else it is, civilization is a mixed bag. It is the old
story of the glass—bag?—being half full and half empty, de-
pending on the viewer. It is this situation that leads some to pre-
dict its expansion into a universal civilization and others to want
to do away with the concept, if not the reality, altogether. Paul
Ricoeur writes that "mankind as a whole is on the brink of a single world civilization representing at once a gigantic progress for
everyone and an overwhelming task of survival and adapting our
cultural heritage to this new setting."[21] Conversely, the anthropologist Tessa Morris-Suzuki insists that that there must be a
"rethinking which would abandon the overworked concept of
'civilization,' rediscover the history of small societies, and develop
a more sensitive understanding of the complexities and contra-
dictions of culture."[22]

Where in this welter of confusions and ambivalences are we to place ourselves? I take my stand as follows. First, whatever I say here, the persistent invocation of civilization as an ideological construct, characterizing one's own society against the barbarians without, will persist. As numerous quotations have shown, "civilization" has taken on the same role as God in being on "our" side. This political use will not disappear.

Next, if the notion of civilization continues to have meaning, it will be in terms of a global civilization and local cultures. Ricoeur had anticipated this development when he wrote that, although ours is a technical civilization, "technics is not the decisive and fundamental factor; for the source of the spread of technics is the scientific spirit itself. Primarily, this is what unifies mankind at a very abstract and purely rational level, and which, on that basis, endows civilization with its universal character."[23] I have tried to modify this "Enlightenment" view by describing a "sci-tech" global civilization where both the material and the rational can find their place. In such a formulation, there is room for both civilization and culture, that is, the local. There is also the possibility of empirical research into their actual interactions. While recognizing that the notion of "sci-tech" is hardly a neutral one, and that science itself must be suitably problematized, it nevertheless follows from this perspective that the concept of a dialogue of civilizations, although its intentions are laudable, is anachronistic.[24]

Lastly, without embracing Morris-Suzuki's declaration, I would like to argue that the concepts of *both* civilization and culture have lost their usefulness and should be retired *intellectually* (I repeat that they will continue to be used in common discourse). Civilization is one of those great Stonehenge figures looming over our mental landscape. Like its adjacent figure, culture, it is one of the major concepts invented and constructed in the eighteenth century and subsequently elaborated in the course of the development of the social sciences. In the new millennium, it has become a fetish. In the new time-space we have entered, it should not only be "deconstructed" but taken down.

What should be left is the *civilizing process*. Civility cuts across civilizations. It is an ongoing process that focuses on the individual and the groups in which he or she exists. The civilizing of the one is essential for the civilizing of the other, in a reiterative process. The idea of civility can avoid the "essence," the us against them, embodied in the idol of civilization. In earlier statements, I have connected civility with self-reflectivity, one outcome of which was the concept of civilization. Now, in suggesting that we detach civility from that concept, an additional aspect of civility comes into view. Not only self-reflection but self-critique is required. This means an openness to criticism of one's own "civilization" and its ways of thinking, putting into place as best we can the interests of humanity as a complex unity.[25] In deciding on those interests, we need to think in terms of the globe and the species as a whole rather than a single civilization and its particular values.

I am not advocating the destruction of the achievements of civilization, but simply trying to free them from its reified embrace. Global civilization and local cultures as a concept goes one step in this direction. The next step is to recognize that the contents of civilization are either so numerous or so emptied of accepted meaning as to make the construct mainly ideological. We have effectively reached the end of "civilization" as a useful concept. It is time that we aim at going back to being "civilized," but now in a new and expanded sense that encompasses all human beings, everywhere.

Reference Matter

Notes

Preface

1. Bruce Mazlish, "Civilization in a Historical and Global Perspective," *International Sociology* 16, no. 3 (September 2001).

Chapter 1. The Origins and Importance of the Concept of Civilization

1. Paul Cartledge, *The Greeks: A Portrait of Self and Others* (New York: Oxford University Press, 1993), 13 and 37. There is some doubt as to whether Homer actually met Carians, who did not "babble" but rather spoke a non-Indo-European language.

2. Ibid., 156–57.

3. The works that I have particularly relied upon are *Geschichtliche Grundbegriffe. Historisches Lexikon zur politisch-sozialen Sprache in Deutschland,* ed. Otto Brunner, Werner Conze, and Reinhart Koselleck (Stuttgart: Klett-Cotta, 1972–97), vol. 7, entry on "Zivilisation, Kultur" by Jorg Fisch (pp. 679–774). This is a quite extraordinary feat of scholarship, with the emphasis on *Kultur*, befitting a German work; *Civilisation: Le Mot et l'idée,* by Lucien Febvre, Émile [*sic* for Ernest] Tonnelat, Marcel Mauss, and Alfredo Niceforo (Paris: La Renaissance du Livre, 1930), especially the entry on "Civilisation" by Febvre, which, although also looking at culture, has an emphasis, as befitting a French work, on civilization (pp. 1–55); and Jean Starobinski, *Blessings in Disguise; or the Morality of Evil,* tr. Arthur Goldhammer (Cambridge, Mass.: Harvard University Press, 1993; Fr. orig. 1989), 1–34, "The Word Civilization." All three works have extremely useful bibliographies. For a more old-fashioned view of the subject, see the chap-

ter on "Universal Civilization and National Cultures" in Paul Ricoeur, *History and Truth*, tr. Charles A. Kelbley (Evanston, Ill.: Northwestern University Press, 1965).

As is and will be evident, in most of this book, I am restricting my account to Western experience, as formative for the eventual conceptualization of the term "civilization." A less single-minded approach would look at ancient Chinese, Egyptian, and other formulations of the civilized/barbarian distinction as well. Indeed, as my friend Mohammad Tamdgidi argues, to an Islamic or Chinese scholar, the point of where the word "civilization" came from, along with its contents, is likely to be a side issue. What would be important to them is the historical trajectory of their word for civilization in their languages and traditions. This is certainly a legitimate enterprise unto itself. It is obviously not the one I am undertaking here, although the notion does inform my own efforts. My focus is on the Western neologism "civilization" and the way in which it has come to exercise hegemony in the modern world, with much attention, however, to a critique of both the concept and its political uses.

4. Febvre et al., *Civilisation: Le Mot et l'idée*, op. cit., 4.

5. *L'Ami des hommes*, pt. 1, 377. The text cited here is from the Gallica website of the Bibliothèque nationale de France, http:// visualiseur.bnf.fr/Visualiseur?Destination=Gallica&O=NUMM-89089 (accessed May 4, 2004). The next two quotations are from pt. 2, 468, and pt. 3, 238. My colleague Jeff Ravel has been helpful in refining the translations used here.

6. Starobinski, *Blessings in Disguise*, 1 and 3.

7. Cf. Almut Höfert, "The Order of Things and the Discourse of the Turkish Threat: The Conceptualisation of Islam in the Rise of Occidental Anthropology in the Fifteenth and Sixteenth Centuries," in *Between Europe and Islam: Shaping Identity in Transcultural Space*, ed. Almut Höfert and Armando Salvatore (Brussels: Presses interuniversitaires européennes, 2000), 67.

8. Cf. various of Claude Blanckaert's works.

9. C. Stephen Jaeger, *The Origins of Courtliness: Civilizing Trends*

and the Formation of Courtly Ideals, 939–1210 (Philadelphia: University of Pennsylvania Press, 1995), 12.

10. *New York Review of Books,* October 7, 1999, 42.

11. For a different translation of this passage from Immanuel Kant's "Idea for a Universal History with a Cosmopolitan Intent" (1784), see *The Philosophy of Kant,* ed. Carl J. Friedrich (New York: Modern Library, 1949), 126.

12. Starobinski, *Blessings in Disguise,* 3.

13. Ibid., 32.

14. Dugald Stewart, *Account of the Life and Writings of Adam Smith,* in *The Collected Works of Dugald Stewart,* quoted in Mary Poovey, *A History of the Modern Fact* (Chicago: University of Chicago Press, 1998), 221.

15. C.-F. Volney, *Éclaircissement sur les États-Unis,* quoted in Febvre et al., *Civilisation,* 50. My colleague Gilberte Furstenberg has been most helpful in getting this translation right.

16. David Warren Sabean, *Power in the Blood: Popular Culture and Village Discourse in Early Modern Germany* (Cambridge: Cambridge University Press, 1984), 29–30.

17. Samuel Huntington, *The Clash of Civilizations and the Remaking of the World Order* (New York: Simon & Schuster, 1996), 43. Although Huntington's definition of civilization is useful, his understanding of the subject is superficial and essentialist.

18. Mehdi Mozaffari, "Can a Declined Civilization Be Reconstructed? Islamic Civilization or Civilized Islam?" *International Relations* 14, no. 3 (December 1998): 31.

Chapter 2. Civilization as Colonial Ideology

1. *Frontiers in Question,* ed. Daniel Power and Naomi Standen (New York: St. Martin's Press, 1999), x.

2. Ibid., 24.

3. Ibid., 36.

4. Ibid., 237, 243.

5. J. H. Elliott, *The Old World and the New, 1492–1650* (Cam-

bridge: Cambridge University Press, 1970), ix. The next quotation is on p. 44.

6. Ibid., 26.

7. Ibid., 103.

8. Quoted in ibid., 73.

9. For further reflections on this general development, see Bruce Mazlish, *The Uncertain Sciences* (New Haven: Yale University Press, 1998), esp. 29 and passim.

10. The edition I am using for convenience is *Captain Cook's Voyages: 1768–1779* (hereafter *Voyages*), selected and introduced by Glyndwr Williams (London: Folio Society, 1997), 151. The introduction offers a short commentary on the textual problems. The next quotation is also from p. 151.

11. Ibid., 81.

12. Ibid., 174. The next two quotations are on pp. 175 and 361. For Zadig's method, see further Carlo Ginzburg, "Morelli, Freud, and Sherlock Holmes: Clues and Scientific Method," in *The Sign of Three: Dupin, Holmes, Peirce*, ed. Umberto Eco and Thomas Sebeok (Bloomington: Indiana University Press, 1983), as well as Mazlish, *Uncertain Sciences*, 8, which also offers additional references.

13. *Captain Cook's Voyages*, ed. Williams, 3. The next quotation is on p. 2.

14. Ibid., 41.

15. Ibid., 233.

16. Ibid., 244.

17. Ibid., 400. The next quotation is from p. 77.

18. Ibid., 208.

19. Ibid., 62.

20. Ibid., 470.

21. Quoted in Hugo West, "The Limits of Enlightenment Anthropology: Georg Forster and the Tahitians," *History of European Ideas* 10, no. 2 (1989): 147. The next quotations are on pp. 148 and 152.

22. Quoted in László Kontler, "Savages Noble and Ignoble: Civili-

zation and Race in George Forster's 'Voyage Round the World' (1777)" (MS), 5.

23. Quoted in West, "Limits of Enlightenment Anthropology," 147–48.

24. Quoted in Kontler, "Savages Noble and Ignoble," 1.

25. James R. Pusey, "Confessions of a Chinese History Teacher: Reflections on the 200th Anniversary of the Macartney Mission" (MS), 11. I have found this an invaluable work.

26. Robert Markley, "Civility, Ceremony, and Desire at Beijing: Sensibility and the European Quest for 'Free Trade' with China in the Late Seventeenth Century," in *Passionate Encounters in a Time of Sensibility*, ed. Maximillian E. Novak and Anne Mellor (Newark: University of Delaware Press, 2000), 64 and 76.

27. Quoted in Pusey, "Confessions of a Chinese History Teacher," 14.

28. Quotations are from *An Embassy to China: Being the Journal Kept by Lord Macartney During his Embassy to the Emperor Ch'ien-lung*, ed. J. L. Cranmer-Byng (Hamden, Conn.: Archon Books, 1963), 124, 188, 264, 125, 191, 225, 228, 215, and 219. One reason the Chinese did not appreciate the European globes was that China was not allotted a big enough space on them, as well as not being shown at the center of the world.

29. Quoted in Pusey, "Confessions of a Chinese History Teacher," 35.

Chapter 3. Civilization as European Ideology

1. Edmund Burke, *Reflections on the Revolution in France*, ed. Thomas H. D. Mahoney (New York: Liberal Arts Press, 1955), 89.

2. Boswell, *Johnson*, as cited in the *OED*, xxv.

3. François Guizot, *History of Civilization in Europe*, tr. William Hazlitt (London: Penguin Books, 1997), 12. Are facts, however, self-evident? For challenges to this view, see Ludwig Fleck, *Genesis and Development of a Scientific Fact*, tr. Fred Bradley and Thaddeus J. Trenn

(Chicago: University of Chicago Press, 1979; Ger. orig. 1935), and Mary Poovey, *A History of the Modern Fact* (Chicago: University of Chicago Press, 1998).

4. Guizot, *History of Civilization in Europe*, 12–13.

5. Ibid., 16.

6. Ibid., 13. The next quotation is from p. 55. In regard to this last citation, we should note that it reflects a view that is still a staple of much present-day Western analysis of Islam.

7. Ibid., 32.

8. Ibid., 11. The next quotation is from p. 17.

9. Ibid., 245.

10. Alexis de Tocqueville, *The European Revolution & Correspondence with Gobineau*, tr. John Lukacs (Garden City, N.Y.: Doubleday, 1959), 224, 227, and 229.

11. Ibid., 248.

12. It should also be noted that Tocqueville has a chapter in the first volume of his *Democracy in America* on race, specifically on the Indians, blacks, and whites.

13. Gobineau, *Pages choisies du comte de Gobineau*, with introd. by Jacques Morland (Paris: Société du "Mercure de France," 1905), 18.

14. Arthur comte de Gobineau, *Inequality of Human Races*, tr. Adrian Collins (New York: H. Fertig, 1967, 1999), ix. The next quotations are from pp. xii and 1.

15. Ibid., 4.

16. Ibid., 27, 56, and 210.

17. Ibid., 77.

18. Gobineau, *Pages choisies*, 36.

19. Quoted in Susanna Barrows, *Distorting Mirrors: Visions of the Crowd in Late Nineteenth-Century France* (New Haven: Yale University Press, 1981), 169. The quotation that follows is from p. 165.

20. Catherine Hall, *Civilising Subjects: Metropole and Colony in the English Imagination, 1830–1867* (Cambridge: Polity Press, 2002), is an interesting exploration especially of the role of missionary groups in fostering the culture of race, although the author limits herself to England

and operates on the terrain of empirical data rather than grand theory such as Gobineau's.

21. Charles Darwin, *The Voyage of the Beagle* (London: J. M. Dent & Sons, 1960), 195.

22. Ibid., 203.

23. Charles Darwin, *The Descent of Man*, in *The Origin of Species and The Descent of Man* (New York: Modern Library, n.d.), 919.

24. Darwin, *Voyage of the Beagle*, 198. The quotations that follow are from pp. 229 and 219.

25. Ibid., 219.

26. *The Autobiography of Charles Darwin and Selected Letters*, ed. Francis Darwin (New York: Dover Publications, 1958), 37.

27. Darwin, *Descent of Man*, 390.

28. Ibid., 500.

29. Ibid., 505.

30. Darwin, *Autobiography*, 69.

Chapter 4. The Civilizing Process

1. John Stuart Mill, *Essays on Politics and Culture*, ed. Gertrude Himmelfarb (Garden City, N.Y.: Doubleday 1963), 151.

2. Ibid., 45.

3. John Stuart Mill, *Principles of Political Economy*, ed. J. M. Robson, 2 vols. (Toronto: University of Toronto Press, 1965), 2: 261.

4. Mill, *Essays*, 126.

5. John Stuart Mill, *On Liberty*, ed. Alburey Castell (New York: Appleton-Century-Crofts, 1947), 94.

6. This statement is called into question, or at least qualified, by Jennifer Pitts, in her "Empire and Social Criticism: Burke, Mill, and the Abuse of Colonial Power" (paper prepared for delivery at the 2002 Annual Meeting of the American Political Science Association), where she remarks that Mill "tended to regard colonial subjects as objects of administration rather than participants in a political process" (30). Mill also seems to have been obtuse in regard to the racial aspects of colonialism.

7. J. S. Mill, *On Liberty and Considerations on Representative Government*, ed. R. B. McCallum (Oxford: Basil Blackwell, 1948), 313.

8. Mill, *Essays*, 135.

9. Sigmund Freud, *Totem and Taboo*, tr. James Strachey (New York: Norton, 1962), 97.

10. Sigmund Freud, *Civilization and Its Discontents*, tr. James Strachey (New York: Norton, 1962), 80.

11. Freud's final title uses the German word *Unbehagen*, which means discontent, uneasiness, or malaise. Originally, he had written *Unglück*, meaning distress, woe, or unhappiness.

12. Sigmund Freud, *The Interpretation of Dreams*, tr. James Strachey (London: George Allen & Unwin, 1961), 548.

13. Sigmund Freud, *Moses and Monotheism*, tr. Katherine Jones (New York: Vintage Books, 1958), 68.

14. Sigmund Freud, *An Autobiographical Study*, tr. James Strachey (New York: Norton, 1963), 138.

15. Sigmund Freud, *The Future of an Illusion*, tr. W. D. Robson-Scott (Garden City, N.Y.: Doubleday, 1964), 66 and 79.

16. Freud, *Civilization and Its Discontents*, 69.

17. Norbert Elias, *The Civilizing Process*, tr. Edmund Jephcott, vol. 1: *The Development of Manners* (New York: Urizen Books, 1978); vol. 2: *Power and Civility* (New York: Pantheon Books, 1982).

18. Quoted in Stephen Mennell, *Norbert Elias: Civilization and the Human Self-Image* (Oxford: Basil Blackwell, 1989), 72. This is a splendid book on Elias, adding its own ideas on civilization and social theory to those of its subject.

19. Quoted in Jan Gorak, "The Rise of Civilization: Scottish Contribution to Enlightenment. Glasgow April 2001" (MS), 4.

20. Mennell, *Norbert Elias*, 35 and 111.

Chapter 5. Other Civilizations

1. William C. Hayes, *The Scepter of Egypt*, vol. 1: *From the Earliest Times to the End of the Middle Kingdom* (New York: Abrams for Metropolitan Museum of Art), 11. I found this a very useful book.

2. For details of how the use of dynasties was established, see ibid., 35ff.

3. Ibid., 78.

4. Tessa Morris-Suzuki, "Rewriting History: Civilization Theory in Contemporary Japan," *positions* 1, no. 2 (1993): 527–28, 531.

5. Kuwabara Takeo, *Japan and Western Civilization. Essays on Comparative Culture*, ed. Katō Hidetoshi (Tokyo: University of Tokyo Press, 1983), 134.

6. See Irokawa Daikichi, *The Culture of the Meiji Period*, tr. and ed. Marius B. Jansen (Princeton: Princeton University Press, 1985), 59, 61. This is an essential text on the Japanese Enlightenment. The other is Carmen Blacker, *The Japanese Enlightenment: A Study of the Writings of Fukuzawa Yukichi* (Cambridge: Cambridge University Press, 1964). As Blacker informs us, "Soon after the Meiji Restoration a group of scholars began to declare that guns, battleships and a new form of government were not in themselves enough. It was also necessary to understand the ideas which in the West had led to the appearance of these things and institutions" (xi). In the formulation by Fukuzawa, civilization was not a matter of things, but of the way people thought: "This supremely important thing we must call the spirit of civilization." At the core of this spirit, for him, was what he characterized as "independence" (31).

7. The quotation about Guizot is from Rumi Sakamoto, "Japan, Hybridity and the Creation of Colonialist Discourse," *Theory, Culture & Society* 13, no. 2 (August 1996): 117.

8. Quoted in Blacker, *Japanese Enlightenment*, 68.

9. Gerrit W. Gong, *The Standard of "Civilization" in International Society* (Oxford: Clarendon Press, 1984), 170. This is a superb book.

10. Ibid., 183.

11. Morris-Suzuki, "Rewriting History," 536.

12. Kuwabara Takeo, *Japan and Western Civilization: Essays on Comparative Culture*, ed. Katō Hidetoshi (University of Tokyo Press, 1983), 119, 129.

13. Dominic Sachsenmaier, "Zhu Zongyuan and the Problem of

Christianity's Foreign Origin" (paper prepared for Conference, Europe in China III, Berlin, April 22–26, 1998, 1–2).

14. China did, in fact, incorporate elements of other civilizations into its own, including both technical innovations and spiritual ones, such as Buddhism.

15. Thongchai Winichakul, "The Quest for '*Siwilai*': A Geographical Discourse of Civilizational Thinking in the Late Nineteenth and Early Twentieth-Century Siam," *Journal of Asian Studies* 59, no. 3 (August 2000): 528–31.

16. See for further details Christina Klein, *Cold War Orientalism: Asia in the Middle Brow Imagination, 1945–1961* (Berkeley: University of California Press, 2003).

Chapter 6. The Dialogue of Civilizations in a Global Epoch

1. Michael Adas, *Machines as the Measure of Men: Science, Technology, and Ideologies of Western Dominance* (Ithaca, N.Y.: Cornell University Press, 1989).

2. *New York Times*, December 16, 1999, A12.

3. Samuel P. Huntington, "The Clash of Civilizations?" *Foreign Affairs* 72, no. 3 (Summer 1993), and *The Clash of Civilizations and the Remaking of the World Order* (New York: Simon & Schuster, 1996). In his article, "The Discourse of Civilization and Pan-Asianism," *Journal of World History* 12, no. 1 (2001), Prasenjit Duara speaks of earlier "Japanese military-sponsored ideas of 'clash of civilization.'" (125).

4. *Economist*, August 18, 2001, 33.

5. *New York Times*, November 10, 2001, A3.

6. See Mehdi Mozaffari, "Can a Declined Civilization Be Reconstructed? Islamic Civilization or Civilized Islam?" *International Relations* 4, no. 3 (December 1998): 33. I am also indebted to Angela Jaffray for Arabic synonyms for the word "civilization."

7. Arnold Toynbee, *Civilization on Trial*, quoted in Mozaffari, "Can a Declined Civilization Be Reconstructed?" 35.

8. Mozaffari, "Can a Declined Civilization Be Reconstructed?" 40.

9. Aziz al-Azmeh, "Barbarians in Arab Eyes" (MS), 2.

10. Personal communication from Mohammad Tamdgidi, March 27, 2000. I owe much to Tamdgidi both as to details of Islamic civilization and to matters of perspective, where he has tried to save me from an overly Western point of view.

11. Muhammad Khatami, *Hope and Challenge: The Iranian President Speaks* (Binghamton, N.Y.: Institute of Global Cultural Studies: Binghamton University, 1997), 1.

12. Ibid., 2–3.

13. Ibid., 11, 28.

14. Ibid., 83.

15. Ibid., 9, 61.

16. See "Auch die Tradition ist nicht ewig: Eine Gesellschaft, die nicht nachdenkt, ist verloren," *Frankfurter Allgemeine Zeitung*, August 1, 1998.

17. *Ettela'at*, November 11, 1999.

18. See Bruce Mazlish, "The Hidden Khomeini," in id., *The Leader, the Led, and the Psyche* (Hanover, N.H.: University Press of New England, for Wesleyan University Press, 1990), esp. 146.

19. *Iran Times*, November 5, 1999, 1.

20. This description is derived from Bruce Mazlish, "Introduction," in *Conceptualizing Global History*, ed. id. and R. Buultjens (Boulder, Colo.: Westview Press, 1993), 1–2.

21. Robert W. Cox, "Civilization and the 21st Century: Some Theoretical Considerations" (paper prepared for the Third Pan-European International Relations Conference, Vienna, September 16–19, 1998), 8, quoted in Mehdi Mozaffari, "Mega Civilization: Global Capital and New Standard of Civilization" (MS, October–November 1999), 20.

22. Quoted in Michael Valdez Moses, *The Novel and the Globalization of Culture* (New York: Oxford University Press, 1995), front matter.

23. *Between Europe and Islam: Shaping Identity in Transcultural Space*, ed. Almut Höfert and Armando Salvatore (Brussels: Presses interuniversitaires européennes, 2000), 22, 68.

24. Wolf Schafer has been at the forefront of arguing for the notion of global civilization and local cultures and was the guiding force in arranging the 1992 conference on that topic.

25. Quoted in Neal Swerdlow, "An Essay on Ancients and Moderns, with a Consideration of Jonathan Swift on Science" (paper given at the Harvard History of Science Center, April 4, 2000), 21.

26. Quoted in Krishan Kumar, *1989: Revolutionary Ideas and Ideals* (Minneapolis, University of Minnesota Press, 2001), 81.

27. Quoted in *International Herald*, September 30, 1999, 4. In fact, some aspects of globalization can legitimately be viewed as part of a neo-colonialism, a new way of subjugating the non-West. As with homogenization/heterogeneity and similar binaries, however, we must not fall into the trap of mistaking parts for the whole.

28. See quotations in Russell Jacoby, "From Utopia to Myopia," *Boston Review*, April–May 1999, 26.

29. Stephen Mennell, "The Globalization of Human Society as a Very Long-term Social Process: Elias's Theory," *Theory, Culture & Society* 7 (1990): 369.

Chapter 7. Conclusions

1. Bernard Lewis, "Culture and Modernization in the Middle East," *IWM Newsletter* 66, August–October 1999, 10.

2. *New York Times*, July 30, 2002, D1.

3. Prasenjit Duara, "The Discourse of Civilization and Pan-Asianism," *Journal of World History* 12, no. 1 (2001): 1.

4. Norbert Elias, *The Civilizing Process: The Development of Manners*, tr. Edmund Jephcott (New York: Urizen Books, 1978), 3–4.

5. Henry Mayhew, *London Labour and the London Poor: A Cyclopaedia of the Condition and Earnings of Those That Will Work, Those That Cannot Work, and Those That Will Not Work* (London: G. Woodfall, 1851); Peter Pulzer, "Fog in Channel: Anglo-German Perspectives in the Nineteenth Century" (2000 Annual Lecture, German Historical Institute, London), 8.

6. Quoted in László Kontler, "William Robertson and His German

Audience on European and Non-European Civilisations," *Scottish Historical Review* 80, pt. 1, no. 209, April 2001, 77.

7. It can be seen at http://www.loc.gov/exhibits/treasures/images/at0058d.6s.jpg (accessed June 1, 2004).

8. *New York Times*, July 17, 2002, A6.

9. *Soviet Historical Encyclopedia*, vol. 15 (1974), s.v. "Tsivilizatsiia"; I owe this reference to my colleague Loren Graham.

10. Personal communication from Loren Graham, February 5, 2000.

11. *Economist*, September 16, 2000, 11.

12. *New York Times*, July 21, 2002. The next quotation is from ibid., March 4, 2001, A24.

13. *New York Times*, November 20, 1999, 1. The next quotation is from ibid., September 13, 2000, A13.

14. Raymond Williams, *Keywords* (New York: Oxford University Press, 1976), 76. It is worth noting that Williams restricts his comment to English, even though it characterizes many other languages and the societies that use them.

15. Sigmund Freud, *The Future of an Illusion*, tr. W. D. Robson-Scott (Garden City, N.Y.: Doubleday, n.d.), 3.

16. Ibid., 66.

17. Sigmund Freud, *Civilization and Its Discontents*, tr. James Strachey (New York: Norton, 1962), 81.

18. Ibid., 69.

19. *Nation and Narration*, ed. Homi Bhabha (London: Routledge, 1990), 5.

20. *New York Times*, August 13, 2002, A4.

21. Paul Ricoeur, "Universal Civilization and National Cultures," *History and Truth*, tr. Charles A. Kelbley (Evanston, Ill.: Northwestern University Press, 1965), 271.

22. Tessa Morris-Suzuki, "Rewriting History: Civilizational Theory in Contemporary Japan," *positions* 1, no. 2 (1993): 546.

23. Ricoeur, "Universal Civilization and National Cultures," 271.

24. For extended remarks on the nature of scientific thought, see

Bruce Mazlish, *The Uncertain Sciences* (New Haven: Yale University Press, 1998), passim.

25. This last formulation owes much to my "dialogue" with my colleague M. H. "Behrooz" Tamdgidi. In our exchange, he warns that the call for the retirement of the term "civilization" may be perceived as an exercise of power by a dominant civilization, dismissing the voices of those in asymmetrical positions in the process of globalization. He also contends that self-reflectivity is not unique to the West, an argument of his that has driven me to make more explicit the differences in the historical context surrounding the neologism "civilization" as contrasted with earlier forms of self-reflectivity.

Index

In this index an "f" after a number indicates a separate reference on the next page, and an "ff" indicates separate references on the next two pages. A continuous discussion over two or more pages is indicated by a span of page numbers, e.g., "57–59."